Meat Me in Manhattan

A Carnivore's Guide to New York

Meat Me in Manhattan

A Carnivore's Guide to New York

©2004 by Josh Ozersky
All Rights Reserved

Published in New York City
by Gamble Guides

Gamble Guides is an imprint of
Ig Publishing
www.igpub.com

ISBN 0-9703125-7-1

10 9 8 7 6 5 4 3 2 1

Photography by Kate Gardner
Book interior design by Joseph Tullman

Meat Me in Manhattan
A Carnivore's Guide to New York

Mr. Cutlets

A Gamble Guide

Ig Publishing, New York

TABLE OF CONTENTS

As I entered the corridor again, a broad meat-like man, in an apron, accosted me, and jerking his thumb over his shoulder said —"Is that your friend?"

"Yes."

"Does he want to starve? If he does, let him live on the prison fare, that's all."

Thinking it would prove of benefit to the scrivener, I acquiesced; and asking the grub-man his name, went up with him to Bartleby.

"Bartleby, this is Mr. Cutlets; you will find him very useful to you."

- Herman Melville,
"Bartleby, the Scrivener"

Meating Mr. Cutlets

Manhattan, taken as a meat capital, is underappreciated. Though our idioms echo in the heartland, and hipsters look to us for the latest dance step or body modification, the smell of our beef, pork, and veal seldom waft far past the borough limits. The plump Chicagoland burgher, sitting smugly in his Zagat-rated steak house, dismisses the Big Apple as a no-man's-land of salads and skinless chicken breasts. The rough-hewn Texan, serving up a whole steer to 1,100 of his closest friends, likewise derides us as little better than vegans. Even the Boston "chowdahead," sweating his beer and burger into a "Broons" T-shirt, has a bad word to say about the way we eat. But with all due respect to Houston, Paris, and Buenos Aires, New York is the great melting pot of meat, from snout to tail, from hoof to horn, boiled and braised, as stews and sandwiches, in every imaginable form.

Unhappily, though, few New Yorkers know much about what the city has to offer. Even within the confines of Manhattan, most meat-eaters, lethargic from their last meal and impatient for the next, tend to drag themselves only as far as their immediate neighborhood. Sluggish, but with a bright twinkle in their jaundiced eyes, they lurch to the same sure bets week after week. Of the city's more marginal meats, its muttons and rotis and empanadas, what they don't know could fill volumes. But they want to learn; they know on some instinctive plane that they are missing out on a sublime char siu (barbecued pork), its ruby and black richness shimmering beneath a honey glaze, somewhere in Chinatown. They've heard of the famous Shanghai juicy buns, the pressed pernil (fresh ham) sandwiches, the Vietnamese phô soups that ornament lower Manhattan. If only they knew where to find them! West-siders wandering blindly through Yorktown, and East Villagers marooned in midtown, likewise scan wildly around, looking for a safe harbor in which to replenish much-needed protein. Seldom do they find it, and end up instead gnawing a carrot at some salad bar, or nibbling sullenly on sushi. It is to keep this from happening that Mr. Cutlets came into the world.

Visitors, too, will find Mr. Cutlets' guide indispensable. Every day, they pour into the city for work and pleasure, with little to go on but word of mouth, a recent Times review, or an overpriced steak house's hype. Couldn't these visitors use a portly old friend, a veteran of countless hours at the chop-table, to guide them in the ways of meat?

It's not enough, however, for Mr. Cutlets merely to point, Zagat-style, to the local highlights for each neighborhood. What good does that do anybody? By concentrating on given meat, Mr. Cutlets can educate and illustrate, making better citizens for a better world, and in the process give much-needed background on the places I recommend. Too many guides give a restaurant a few breezy superlatives and leave it at that. But why is that fried chicken "outstanding" or the meat loaf "tough to beat"? And what does the writer consider good fried chicken? These are things a person reading a guidebook has a right to know.

Lastly, a word to prospective troublemakers. Mr. Cutlets is an opinionated old coot, whose ex cathedra pronouncements and dogmatic decrees may rub some people the wrong way. But I make no apology. The faux-populist thrust of so many current guides is nothing less than a key to chaos. Although the focus group and write-in vote may be sweet and fitting to marketing executives and Family Feud contestants, it's not Mr. Cutlets' way. My carcass has been spent in the service of my readers; I therefore submit my guide to the hands of the people with tranquility, my conscience as clear as consommé, my opinions unrepentant and undisguised.

Mr. Cutlets

June 2003

A Note on Ratings

Meat Me in Manhattan includes some traditional reviews, which Mr. Cutlets has provided for the guidance of the young and the convenience of the old. In the interest of convention (and commerce), I have rated each restaurant with easy-to-remember icons. These ratings are based on the star system devised by the Michelin Company a century ago. The celestial wisdom of Michelin has been universally regarded as the first, best system for rating restaurants, and that's good enough for me. Why reinvent the wheel? As in la guide rouge, values are expressed primarily in terms of convenience.

Good, But Not Great Interesting mostly for academic or nutritional purposes.

Neighborhood Favorite Eat there if you happen to be nearby.

Worth a Detour Good enough to merit going out of your way.

Destination Meal A meal to plan an evening around, or even a trip. A true meat mecca.

I break with Michelin in not taking service, setting, number of tables, or other nonfood factors into consideration. Quality of Carnivorous Experience alone informs these ratings. I have also assigned a cost rating to each restaurant, which loosely translates as follows:

Inexpensive Under $15

Affordable Between $15 and $30 per person, all told, depending on alcohol

Moderately Expensive Between $30 and $50 per person

Expensive Prodigious prices; brace yourself for a soaking

1 Frequently Asked Questions About Meat

What is meat?

To carnivores, meat is the morning sun and the evening star. It is a sausage at sunrise, a sandwich at noon, and a steak late at night. . . .

No, no. I mean what does meat mean? Does it include chicken? Fish?

Meat is a broad word, that generally has been used to mean the muscles, organs, and (in some cases) the extremities of various animals, particularly birds and mammals. It doesn't include fish, crustaceans, mollusks, or creeping things. And it doesn't include bones, beaks, or feathers. Still, that leaves a pretty wide swath of the natural world. You could make a good argument for including fish, since they are animals too, and a thick tuna or swordfish steak is a more substantial, meat-like meal than (say) a spitted lark, or a paper-thin slice of prosciutto. But the tradition descends from Catholic Europe and its classification of Lenten foods. By the time gastronomy attained the rank of a science, fish and eggs were allowed, but meat wasn't, and that's the way it still stands, at least as far as semantics go.

What are the different kinds of meat?

The meat kingdom breaks down as follows:

Game meats are those animals that live in the wild until they are shot or trapped by hunters. The most common of these are rabbit, venison (deer), and game birds such as duck and pheasant. Game meat tends to vary according to region. It can be as exotic as alligator or rattlesnake, as in Florida, or as familiar as the squirrels Georgians still use as the traditional basis for Brunswick stew. For obvious reasons, game tends to be less available and more expensive than those meats manufactured by husbandry for slaughter. This should translate to their flesh being better tasting; but, unhappily, it isn't. Game tends to be dry and stringy, as the animals actually use their muscles rather than standing around waiting to be turned into meat.

Domesticated birds are called poultry.

The most typical livestock are sheep, pigs, cows, chickens, turkeys, and (outside America) goats, horses, and pigeons. In recent years, fat-conscious breeders have started to develop ostriches and buffalo, but that is still a niche market for upscale consumers.

Organ or variety meats include liver, sweetbreads (pancreas), and brains.

Offal is parts of the animal too foul to serve in and of themselves, but too good to throw out. They end up in scrapple, some sausages, headcheese, souse, and other gnarly products that hardly anyone eats anymore outside of Pennsylvania.

What about the special meat diseases I've read so much about? How can I avoid E. coli, trichinosis, mad cow disease, and other animolecules?

A fair question! After all, you can't very well enjoy a meal if you are writhing in an intensive care unit. But there isn't much chance of getting any of these diseases unless you are butchering your own meat, or taking all your meals in dumpsters. Still, there is at least a theoretical threat of disease.

E. coli is a germ that lives inside your own body, but an evil cousin is sometimes found in tainted meat; most often, it shows up in low-grade hamburger, of the kind they made you eat in junior high. You can kill potential E. coli germs by overcooking all your meat (160 degrees F is recommended).

Trichinosis is a life-threatening illness caused by trichinae, a parasitic nematode (roundworm) that lives in corrupted pork. The disease arose when it was common to feed pigs on garbage; half a century of federal regulation and scientific husbandry has banished trichinosis to the compost heap of history. Fewer than fifty people a year get trichinosis, and the majority of those get it from eating bears and other trophy animals. Even if by some chance you did take home a trichinae-infested pork chop, the tiny predators within it would be killed as soon as the internal temperature reached 140 degrees—more than cool enough for pork to stay juicy and delicious.

Mad cow disease is pretty much a British issue, so unless you are going to England, or an epidemiology conference, don't pay it a second thought.

There are other meat diseases—food poisoning, botulism, and so forth, but generally, our meat is among the healthiest in the world, especially once it's been cleaned and cooked.

There is one particular disease that meat-eaters are vulnerable to, but it deserves special treatment, since it is as much an accomplishment as it is a complaint. I am speaking of gout, "the king of diseases and the disease of kings." For many years, Mr. Cutlets thought gout to be a kind of semi-imaginary Dickensian ailment, like the dropsy or the vapors. But it's very real, a kind of specialized arthritis caused by an excess of uric acid in the blood. Its most common symptom is an exquisite tenderness in the foot, which prevents the sufferer from moving—though not from eating. Still, one bout of gout is enough for boasting purposes, and it is easily cured by a common medication. One can also avoid it by drinking plenty of water.

What are some of the major ways meat is prepared before cooking?

It depends on what you're trying to do. Chefs marinate meat, rub spices into it, lard it with garlic slivers, hit it with hammers, and so on. But the major transformative processes all take a lot more time and effort, and usually happen before you ever see the meat in the market.

Aging is done in two ways. In dry aging, a piece of meat, usually prime beef, is left in a cool, dry place to sit out in the air for several weeks. In that time, it loses up to a quarter of its weight and gains correspondingly in flavor. In wet aging, they seal up the steak with some kind of chemicals in a space-age vacuum container called a Cryovac. The meat emerges from this plastic cocoon some time later, unnaturally tender, and with its flavor also improved somewhat. Wet aging isn't as good as dry, but it's cheaper, and so most restaurants (and casinos and cruise ships) use it. But the shortcut always tells.

Other preparations derive from historical techniques for preserving meats before refrigeration. Air-drying is self-explanatory, ancient, and uninteresting. Curing consists of taking a piece of meat, such as a pork belly, rubbing lots of salt into it (along with some sugar and other spices), and leaving it to dry out. Back in the day, this was the primary means by which meat was preserved, but it's still done today to make ham, bacon, and other tasty meat-treats. Brining or pickling consists of salting meat by immersing it for a long time in a salt-water bath. Corned beef is the most well known brined meat, but many fine restaurants today brine their pork chops and chicken, imparting them with a special sweetness and juiciness. In smoking, fragrant vapors from hardwood embers permeate throughout the meat, breaking down its fibers, flavoring it, and cooking it over a very long period of time. Smoking is the most complicated, difficult, and noble of all modes of meat preparation, and the only one that cooks the meat in the act of preserving it.

So what do the different terms used to describe meat, such as "prime," "Black Angus," and so forth, mean? What is mutton? I'm confused.

Here I must abandon the literary device of the FAQ, with its docile imaginary catechumen. There is a lot to say about meat, too much so to constrain within the conventions of a FAQ. What follows is a thumbnail sketch of the major kinds of meat, meant to provide basic background knowledge for curious carnivores.

Beef—"the best, the most fortifying, and the most nourishing of all butcher's meat," according to the Larousse Gastronomique—is made from various breeds of bovine animals, including oxen, steers, bulls, cows, and heifers. Let's go through these one by one. Oxen are castrated bovine males; steers are males castrated before puberty, when impure thoughts spoil their taste. Most of the beef we eat comes from steers. Bulls are uncastrated bovine males, and taste as mean as they act. Cows are bovine females who have had a baby; mature females who haven't had one yet are called heifers. The baby is called a calf, and can be of either sex. Calves grow up (or rather, don't grow up) to become veal.

There are different breeds of bovine cattle, which have been engineered as carefully and deliberately as dog breeds, both for milking and eating. Among the most popular of the latter in America are Angus (both black and red), Hereford, and Shorthorn. There are also European and Asian breeds of cattle, such as the French Limousin, or the Japanese Wagyu, which rival or surpass even the very best American beef, depending on whom you talk to. Most people agree that Black Angus cattle are the tastiest, most well-marbled beef you can buy. The American Angus Association certifies beef as Angus; many restaurants and butchers claim to serve Angus beef, but only the certification—and the taste—proves it.

Beyond cattle breeding, the most important factor informing the taste and texture of your steak is what the animal is fed. Wagyu (Kobe) beef tastes funny to Americans partially because of the strange beer-based diet of these animals; our beef is generally fed on grain. Artisanal beef from a family farm or top-flight ranch tends to have a different and better taste, because of the sweet clover and alfalfa they get in their diet, as opposed to the processed, drug-and-chemical-spiked corn feed given to their unfortunate brothers in some agribusiness mills.

Beef, once killed and butchered, is then graded according to federal guidelines. The best beef is called prime; the next best choice; then select. Amazingly, given how much beef Americans eat, almost none of the steaks, chops, or roasts we eat are less than select. The lower grades (standard, commercial, utility, cutter, and canner) generally go into canned products, pet food, and god knows what else. And that's just the beef that is graded; there is a lot that is passed as wholesome, but isn't submitted for grading. You can only imagine what that turns into. Anyway, the whole system is somewhat misleading, since it is based not on absolute criteria, but on a sliding scale of arbitrary values (color, marbling, etc.). Today's "prime" rib roast might have been only "choice" or "select" twenty years ago.

Beef has a strong, distinct taste that is very subtle and varies wildly as you eat your way through the carcass. But even the most intensely flavored portions of a good steer, such as the skirt, chuck, and heart are less strongly flavored than even the blandest parts of a sheep or goat. Whether this is because of cattle's immemorial primacy as the main source of meat for Western people, or because its taste is hard-wired into us Americans, is impossible to say. But the range, richness, and complexity of beef, particularly when carefully aged and judiciously cooked, give it a preeminent place among the orders of meat.

The most popular cuts are the short loin, which produces shell steaks and tenderloin (filet); the ribs, which make rib steaks and standing rib roasts, and which are frequently, although erroneously, called "prime rib"; sirloin, from which many fine steaks come, and chuck, the home of the best hamburgers; and such intensely tasty, beefy cuts as short ribs (flanken); the skirt, or "Roumanian tenderloin"; the flank (London broil); and the tail (oxtail).

Veal are immature cattle in their first year. Their tender flesh and delicate flavor comes from their immaturity, and also from the fact that they nurse for a long time. "Milk-fed" veal, when it actually has fed on milk and not on some weird soy concoction or formula, has a pale pink color and an amazingly full and vibrant yet mild taste. A good piece of veal should have as much flavor, in its own quiet way, as a good shell steak. Of course, not all veal is milk-fed. "Bob" veal, a cheaper form taken from calves less than a week old, is seldom seen, but watch out for it, as it is truly nasty. The best cut of veal is generally the rib chop, which is exquisitely rich and tender, and so good that even the most ostentatious chefs know better than to do anything with it but stick it under a hot broiler. The loin chops, loin roast, and leg are also good, as is the veal breast, especially when slow-cooked, with or without a stuffing. Scaloppini are very thin slices, carefully cut from the leg, diaphanously tender, pale, pink, and with almost no external fat. People who don't particularly like meat are crazy about scaloppini, which tells you something about both it and them. Everything you have heard about the short, grim lives of calves is true, at least as far as commercial veal is concerned.

Pork is the meat of pigs. Pork isn't graded by the USDA, nor do the breeds matter much. It is more delicate in flavor than beef, but also rich and succulent—although less so now than in the past. Adult pigs are called hogs; a female who has had her first litter is called a sow. Both hogs and sows are eaten, as are the little piglets, which are sometimes called sucklings or porkers. Generally, these have an even more delicate taste than do grown animals; maybe too delicate. I'm never excited to eat a suckling pig, although its presentation, whole, as an edible bronze sculpture of itself, is hard to resist. (Give me fresh ham or pork chops instead.) Pork is probably the most popular meat in the entire world, and it's hard not to see why. Pigs are cheap and very easy to raise (in some places you don't even need to feed them; you just send them out foraging for themselves). They don't require vast grassy plains to reproduce. As a result, there are more recipes from around the world for pork than for any other meat—jerk pork from Jamaica, char siu from Hong Kong, barbecue in the West Indies, pulled pork in North Carolina—to say nothing of the infinite variety of the pig's secondary products: the bacons, the sausages, the scrapples and pickled pig's feet, the fatback and salami and so many more wonderful, wonderful things. O pig! Mr. Cutlets must genuflect before your vast power.

Nearly every part of the pig can be eaten—"everything but the squeal," as the old hogmen used to say. The most popular roast is the loin, which is sometimes cut up into pork chops. Don't confuse it with the pork tenderloin, a miserable, tasteless cut with none of the loin's complexity, firmness, or succulence. Spareribs have a sweet taste and toothsome resiliency, and are the medium of choice for any kind of barbecue. They have a big knuckle on the end that is sometimes cut off and made into rib tips, in America, or cooked in black bean sauce, by the Chinese. It goes without saying that anybody who is serious about ribs eats spareribs. Back ribs (sometimes cutely called "baby" back ribs) are smaller and more manageable, with grainier, sweeter, tenderer meat, but less overall taste. The rear legs of the pig are called hams, and can be either roasted plainly as "fresh ham" or pernil, or cured and smoked into the familiar salty-sweet form. The picnic shoulder is a big, tough cut with lots of weird muscles and ligaments running at cross patterns. It has to be either slow-smoked or slow-roasted, but when it is, watch out! There's nothing else like it! Bacon is made from the cured and/or smoked belly of the pig. Pork is so tender, and its browned fat so transporting, that very few parts of the pig are ever used for stew. As a meat, something there is about pork that just takes to browning. The crusty skin of pork roasts is so good that people eat it itself, as crackling.

Lamb and mutton come from sheep. Lamb is the immature form, the veal to mutton's beef. Because sheep have much stronger, tougher meat than one finds in pigs or cows, most people today eat lamb exclusively. Many don't even know what mutton is! And yet, if you like the taste of lamb (and who doesn't?), it is only amplified in mutton. Admittedly, the smell and taste can be a little strong, but when roasted or broiled, its opiate fumes intoxicate the nostrils and quicken the heartbeat. (The ancient Greeks would roast sheep under open skies, in the belief that the gods were pleased by the smell of roasting mutton flesh.) Mutton is redder and fattier than beef, and stands up to any number of strong flavors. Algerians cook it with prunes and almonds, Moroccans with lemons and olives, the Belgians with endives, the Swedes with dill—but in no way do these spices ever get in the way of "that muttony goodness." The closest approximation of mutton on lamb is lamb-breast, a fatty cut that is seldom served in restaurants. Lamb, of course, is popular in every country, particularly the delicate rib chops, which can be eaten with the fingers. Lamb shoulders and legs make delicious roasts, particularly when, as in the French boulangerie style, the fat is allowed to drip onto a waiting bed of potatoes and onions, which are perfumed and patinaed as they absorb the excellent nectar. Practically every part of the lamb is good, even the brains.

Like lamb, chicken, turkey, and duck all tend to be eaten in their immature form. And as with mutton, this is a grievous loss to gastronomy. A plump old hen, like a pungent sheep, is in every way more flavorful and interesting than its pallid younger form. "A tough old turkey with plenty of character," wrote A.J. Liebling, "makes the best civet, and only in a civet is turkey good to eat." Young turkey, Liebling opined, "like a young sheep, calf, spring chicken, and baby lobster, is a pale preliminary phase of its species." Likewise, it's unthinkable that any serious eater would want to eat any of these birds without their skins.

Was Meat Me in Manhattan inspired by the Atkins diet? And what is Mr. Cutlets' opinion of this carnivorous craze?

Mr. Cutlets didn't need the late Dr. Atkins to teach him about eating meat. I've been on the Atkins diet since the McKinley administration, and my unconcern for doctors has become proverbial. But Dr. Atkins' diet has undoubtedly been a great boon to humanity, and Mr. Cutlets believes in its precepts to his very core. Essentially, the diet requires its adherents to forswear nearly all carbohydrates. The body, without any physiological cue to create insulin, simply stops producing blood sugars. Lacking any other source of fuel, it dips into its reserves: the unsightly fat encasing the torsos of gourmands. What the body doesn't know is that you are laughing it up, eating bacon like there's no tomorrow, all the while enjoying the weight loss of a long-distance runner.

The only problem with Atkins-induced ketosis (other than the stinky breath, leg cramps, and occasional dizziness) is the outside possibility of getting tired of meat. But no New Yorker should need fear that fate. Our city provides so many wonderful meat options, that one can easily construct a whole regimen of eating that never duplicates a single meat. For example, a person might have Veselka bacon for breakfast, spicy-salt pork chops for lunch, a mid-afternoon snack of Shaller and Weber's Landjaeger sausage, and finish the day with a bisteca florentina with sautéed escarole and a big salad. Does that sound so bad? New York and the Atkins diet were made for each other.

Can I meet Mr. Cutlets?

Mr. Cutlets is a public figure, and is only too happy to oblige the many young people who come to him for advice and direction. He will happily correspond gratis with anyone who writes him at: mister_cutlets@yahoo.com

2 The Burger Barons

Hamburgers, too, have their own collective soul. But like barbecue or mountain flora, the hamburger—the definitive American sandwich, after all—varies from place to place. In L.A., they eat it with weird things on top. In Oklahoma City, burgers are mixed with thick-hewn chopped onions before

grilling. In Austin, the classic flat griddle burger is defined by Dirty Martin's (or at least it was until the health department made Martin's switch to preformed patties—a disaster in burger history comparable to the advent of the Hays Code).

And the New York burger? Unhappily, it has only pathology to mark it. Our burgers are victims of gigantism, grossly oversized atomic mutants that can hardly fit on a bun. Because of the bigger-and-deffer aesthetic that has transformed Manhattan in the last ten years, it was perhaps inevitable that New York bars and restaurants would end up serving fist-shaped hamburgers, more suited to an anaconda's gullet than the table of a true gourmand. But the rent is high in our bars and restaurants; and if you're going to charge someone $7 or $8 for a cheeseburger deluxe platter, the least you can do (or so the thinking goes) is give them a surfeit of meat.

The problem is that, while these meat-planets are filling enough, they defeat the whole idea of a hamburger—or especially a cheeseburger. The hamburger, it will be remembered, didn't used to be considered a substantial meal in and of itself. Cartoon characters with hamburger fetishes, like J. Wellington Wimpy and Jughead Jones, were comical precisely because they had to keep eating hamburgers all day; one burger wouldn't even have been worth their while. Hence their elaborate hamburger-acquiring antics. But the reason they loved hamburgers so was obvious: nothing in the world is like a really good hamburger—or more accurately, a cheeseburger. (For the purposes of this guide, I will be writing exclusively of cheeseburgers, since a hamburger is basically a maimed and naked thing without cheese.)

In its classic form, a toasted or grilled enriched white bun supports (but just barely) a grilled disc of hot meat, absorbing its juice in the process. The disc, which has been deeply browned on either a flat metal griddle or charred by infernal flames, has a slice of yellow American cheese laid across it in the last stages of its cooking—and the contrast between the rough, blackened surface and the smooth, viscous blanket of cheese provides a second level of tension. When you bite into a cheeseburger conceived according to nature, there are five elements that bind together: the delicately seeded outer surface of bun; the airy, unobtrusive sweetness of the inner bun; the soft sea of yellow cheese, so sticky and yielding; and beneath all that, the caramelized crunch flavor of browned meat outside, and the pure beef essence inside, coursing with liquid flavor. That's a cheeseburger! It's a very complex food, one of the greatest of American inventions. Mr. Cutlets ranks it somewhere between the McCormick reaper and penicillin.

So how does the capital city of the American century treat this sandwich? By bloating its centerpiece into grotesque sizes and shapes; by replacing American cheese with revolting Limburgers and bleus; by setting it on leathery five-grain Kaiser rolls, or chewy English muffins; and then loading that with every kind of topping a deranged mind could conceive of, from guacamole to chili. It's an unhappy fate for a sandwich with a history and pedigree of the cheeseburger!

New York's cheeseburgers come in four varieties: grilled, griddled, griddle-braised, and broiled. Grilled burgers are fired over hot flames, and take on an aggressive char, which often works in contrast to the juicy meat within. Today's fat-conscious consumer likes how the juice drips away from the cooking burger; s/he thinks the cook is doing him/her a favor that way. But only chuck is juicy enough to have so much of its precious bodily fluids leeched away by fire, and still be juicy; a grilled sirloin burger is an accident waiting to happen.

VESELKA

There are a number of first-class grilled burgers to be found all over Manhattan. At **Veselka,** on Second Avenue at 9th Street, very fresh meat is formed into irregular discs and grilled over a very hot flame. A thick slice of American cheese fits neatly over the blackened surface, its corners painting the patty's compass points, which extrude slightly from beneath the soft toasted bun. Though the cheese is thick and viscous, the fiery flames assure that it will bind to the blackened burger. The beef is intensely tasty, and its charmingled juices mingle with the wide, toasted bun beneath and the seeded, toasted bun above. All in all, it's soft, tender, intensely flavorful, and exactly the right shape and thickness for its constituent elements. Its fearful symmetries aside, however, what really takes the Veselka burger to the next level is the bacon: thick, soft, rich, smoky-sweet, and twice the size of ordinary slices. It provides an incredible enrichment, and is so soft as to be texturally unobtrusive. I wish I had some now!

Molly's, on 22nd Street at Third Avenue, has a superb ten-ounce burger that resembles Veselka's, but on steroids. Molly's accomplishes this the right way, though, expanding horizontally rather than vertically: you have to hold it with both hands, and only a voracious eater finishes it without a sense of accomplishment. Uptown, the only rival I know of to these two restaurants is the enormously popular **Nick's Burger and Pizza Joint,** on Broadway and 75th Street, and **Nick's Burger and Pizza Joint Too,** on 71st and Columbus Avenue. Nick's meat isn't quite up to the standard of Molly's, Veselka's, and all other great burger shrines, but it is always fresh, and nearly always cooked to order. Nick's is cheap, dependable, and it delivers—but the freshness of the bun isn't always what you're looking for, and only one slice of cheese ornaments the otherwise perfect patty.

The Ear Inn, on Spring Street between Washington and Greenwich, serves an exemplary sirloin burger—less juicy, but with a sharper, more distinct beefy taste. Unhappily, it's served on a too-big bun, and of its general morphology, the less said the better. I like the Ear Inn, but I wouldn't order my last meal there; and that's really the best test of any restaurant. Likewise, **McHale's Bar,** on Eighth Avenue at 46th Street, is in terms of pure taste almost impossible to beat; but the sandwich is so huge and so ill-formed that it's almost impossible to really regard it as a hamburger. It's more like taking a bath in charred-hamburger flavor, with a lot of crunchy bacon thrown in. Which, come to think of it, doesn't sound so bad. But orthodoxy of form has to count for something when you're competing at this level.

While some of New York's most celebrated hamburgers are grilled over fire or charcoal, a number of highly regarded kitchens broil theirs instead. The most famous of these is the **Corner Bistro,** at the junction of West 4th Street and Hudson Street. (It's actually not the junction, due to the weird winding ways of the West Village, but if you make it that far you will see the bar's neon sign on the corner of Jane Street and can navigate by eye from there.) The Corner Bistro is often rated as "the best burger in New York," but I think that is more a piece of received wisdom, like "the sexiest man alive," than a carefully thought-through judgment, like the National Book Award. In any case, the Corner Bistro does have a superb broiled burger. Occasionally, wide-eyed food writers, in the first flush of their encounter with the Corner Bistro, will refer to the burger as "char-broiled." Nothing could be farther from the truth. The whole strength of the CB burger is that it is slowly broiled under a comparatively low fire: as a result, it stays juicier than steak house versions, which emerge from their thousand-degree hells with every drop of precious juice huddled in the middle like frightened refugees.

The less famous **Knickerbocker Bar & Grill,** on University Place at 9th Street, is nearly as good—but drops the ball with its choice of cheese, too-thick patty, and the distraction of a denser bun. And although it is technically not in Manhattan, no discussion of beef would be complete without mention of **Peter Luger Steak House,** the Bayreuth of Beef, on Broadway at Driggs Avenue in Brooklyn. Yes, the temple of steak offers a hamburger on its lunch menu, and at half the cost of some of its rivals. It is made from the same superb short loins as are served in their famous porterhouse steaks, of which more later. Presumably, they grind up the "tail" of the short loin, a dangling comma-shaped object, and serve it as hamburgers so it shouldn't go to waste. Well, this is a benevolent gesture indeed, and meat-men (and meat-women) will surely appreciate it. Unhappily, the kitchen staff isn't as sure-handed with their hamburgers as they are with their steaks, and so wide variations in doneness occasionally come up. Moreover, the rotund shape of the beef, combined with the chewy bun, makes this more of an overture to steak than a hamburger in itself. Which is as it should be: nobody should be going to Peter Luger and leaving without eating steak.

Another name that comes up a lot when people talk about New York's best burgers is actually that of a chain: **Jackson Hole,** with five outposts throughout Manhattan (64th Street between Second and Third Avenues; Madison Avenue between 90th and 91st Streets; Second Avenue between 83rd and 84th Streets; Columbus Avenue at 85th Street; Third Avenue between 34th and 35th Streets). Jackson Hole is undoubtedly the most successful purveyor of "griddle-braised" burgers in New York. The griddle-braised burger is an odd hybrid of hamburgers and pot roast: thick burgers are cooked on a flat griddle with little metal cones covering them.

The result is a disintegrating horror that can barely hold its shape. The sealing-in of all the meat's moisture, however, does ensure your eating an extremely moist sandwich: the griddle-braised burger is so tender that it might even be suitable for the feeding of infants. Jackson Hole doesn't make the mistake of trying to pot-steam too large a mass of meat, though whether this is for admirable aesthetic reasons, or just cheapness, I cannot say. As with the McHale burger, there is something comforting about the sheer carnal decadence of the thing. (As T.E. Lawrence once said, "There seemed a certainty in degradation.") Perhaps the Jackson Hole burger would be the burger of choice for a last meal, when propriety no longer matters and only infantile satisfaction can be salvaged at the gate of destruction. I would hope, though, for better-tasting beef in the face of doom; Jackson Hole sometimes tastes a little gnarly. Two short-order restaurants in the Village use better meat than Jackson Hole for their griddle-braised burgers: **Paul's Palace,** on Second Avenue between 7th and 8th Streets (St. Mark's Place); and nearby **Cozy Soup and Burger,** on Broadway at Astor Place. Since the griddle-braised burger requires no particular skill to make, and is as often as not covered with half a dozen toppings, it isn't hard to find good examples of it all over town.

Having moved through the methods most popular in New York, we come back to the primal mode of making a hamburger: the simple flat metal griddle. The griddle, in Mr. Cutlets' opinion, is the perfect tool for creating a hamburger. First of all, it shouldn't be overly clean. A weary cook may scrub it at the end of the day with a porous brick of pumice, but even if he does an assiduous job, the faint residue of a thousand previous hamburgers will inhere in the metal, and impart their spirit and flavor to every subsequent descendant. Moreover, on a flat metal grill, there is no place for the fat to go: rather than dripping away to oblivion, as with a grill or broiler, or penetrating pressurized vapors back into the meat, as with griddle-braising, the fat is refracted back purely as a browning medium, and should, in theory anyway, caramelize the surface of a disc that is basically all surface anyway.

Joe's Jr., on 12th Street at Avenue of the Americas (Sixth Avenue), is the best of these, although fine versions can be found at diners all around town. For some reason, though, I always have found the best ones to be served in bus stations. Still, for the Manhattanite who really loves the traditional griddled burger, there is only one place to see it in its classical form, replicated with the regularity of hexameters. That

place, of course, is **White Castle** (Eighth Avenue between 37th and 38th Streets), still the original exemplar of the "slider." The White Castle is a minute object, a couple of ounces of low-grade beef scrapple, machine-tooled into a square with five round holes. Although some carpers have (correctly, I suspect) guessed at the real reason for the holes—a way of stealing an extra patty from every four—it also serves an ingenious function: the greasy, oniony steam from the grill floats up through the lacunae, softening the dinner roll they are served on, and refracting back into the hamburger itself. A

White Castle is a brief, intense experience, like a whippet, and cheap too. Five White Castles give you as much hamburger aesthetic in one sitting as you could possibly ask for—unless, like Mr. Cutlets, you find their double cheeseburgers even better. (The double cheeseburger, with two levels of beef and three beef-steamed pieces of white bread, is as rich as cheesecake.) In a city marked by too-big burgers, the White Castle is actually too small to be perfect; but in its thinking and proportions, it's infinitely closer to the Platonic ideal.

Thus ends my discussion of burgers per se. But it would be remiss, even for such a sad figure as Mr. Cutlets, not to wheeze a few last words into the cocked ear of an attentive listener about the city's various interpretations of the hamburger. Yes, though my antique sensibilities chafe at their oddity, Mr. Cutlets has to admit that the various postmodern glosses on the hamburger have their points. The best of these is the chopped hangar steak slider on a bialy, as invented and served at **aKa Cafe** (Clinton Street just south of Stanton Street). The hangar steak, once chopped up and grilled, no longer registers as hangar steak, but just as a coarse, lean burger patty. It's really an inventive sandwich: the aKa slider is as delicate as a soufflé, and has as much structural tension built into it as a geodesic dome. The sandwich-pressed bialy has deep crunch, with a slightly chewy dough—like all good toasted bialys, it reminds you of nothing so much as perfect pizza crust. That crunchiness stands in perfect counterpoint to the softness contained within, particularly as accentuated by a mild, creamy pickle relish that functions as cheese. (Though crunchy, a toasted bialy doesn't get in the way of the load it is bearing; it's like good ciabatta bread in that way, a flying buttress.) The slider is probably a little bit thicker and the meat much more done than it should be; but at least the aKa Cafe tried.

The same can't be said of **21 Club,** on 52nd Street between Fifth and Sixth Avenues. They've been distorting hamburgers since long before more inventive kitchens got in on the game, and their open-faced burger, mixed of sirloin and top round, remains exactly as good as if you bought a lump of ground meat for $20 and broiled it in your underwear while talking on the phone. $20! Yes, that is roughly equal to three times the cost of a Peter Luger burger, and twice the price of Molly's. Even if it were great, could any man of spirit keep that thought from crowding all pleasure from his mind? This does not even factor in the unpleasant quality of the company in 21 Club, which seems to consist largely of sedate septuagenarians in blazers; the days when J.J. Hunsecker held court from a private booth are long gone.

A more contemporary bid for the "ultimate" hamburger has been made very publicly by no less a personage than Daniel Boulud, arguably the city's top chef. At **DB Bistro Moderne,** on 44th Street between Fifth and Sixth Avenues, the hapless hamburger is subjected to the indignity of being disemboweled, filled with braised short ribs, black truffles, and foie gras, and formed into a moonlike shape before being popped onto a fancy bun. Is it possible, I thought, that this sandwich could be as disgusting as it sounds?

I needn't have worried. The burger, which is as round and unwieldy as a cannonball, doesn't taste like anything at all. If black truffles and foie gras are present at all, they hardly register. The middle layer of the burger is braised short ribs, as advertised. But so what? The two tastes and textures, neither of which are particularly striking, don't combine well, and don't taste like they were meant to. It's just another overpriced combo sandwich, an inedible Dagwood whipped up to impress the credulous. Rather than an elevated take on the hamburger by a great chef, the DB burger is merely hermaphroditic: neither haute cuisine nor a good hamburger, it combines the worst elements of both, for an astronomical price.

Probably the best of the high-end burgers can be found at the good steak houses, at **Union Square Cafe** (16th Street at Broadway) and at **Home** (Cornelia Street between Bleecker and West 4th Streets). All these burgers are presentable and well made, use top-flight ground sirloin, and are presented in an unadorned way, albeit on rolls too big and hard. They're all good; they're all reasonably priced for the room; and, taken as ground-beef sandwiches, they are absolutely first-rate. It is only as hamburgers that they fall short; but only the most dogmatic of burger fetishists, like Mr. Cutlets, would hold that against them.

Beacon
25 W. 56th St. | 212.332.0500

Meats of Note: veal chop, shell steak, rib-eye steak

Beef is a bully. Anti-intellectual to its marrow, it resists the blandishments of gourmands, who hope to coax out of it unthought-of flavors. Intensely competitive chefs, ingenious as Batman villains, have exhausted themselves trying to improve upon it. And all to no account. Beef is what it is. If history has taught us anything, it's that you can't do better by beef than to put it near fire, and take it away soon afterward.

This lesson is a painful one to cuisiniers, few of whom are centered enough to relinquish that kind of control. You can imagine their train of thought. "Five years at Lespinasse, and I have to cook steak like some backyard boob? For this I went to the Culinary Institute of America?" Given a free hand, these resentments would result in New York looking like one great Iron Chef battle, with each entrant outdoing the next in rococo embellishments. Happily, market pressure is basically conservative, and will reward that subtle chef who can ride herd on the taste of beef and other robust meats without giving in to hubris.

Wally Malouf, the directing intelligence of Beacon, is one such cook. A shortish, bearded man who radiates energy, Malouf made his bones, so to speak, as the chef of the dynamic Rainbow Room, and in opening Beacon several years ago seemed to some critics to be going backward. But Malouf was ahead of the curve in embracing bold, minimalist fare, a good year before everybody and their brother starting serving hangar steak and short ribs to people who had previously primped for lemongrass salmon. His style, though, was in no way primitive. "For something to truly be simple, you've gone through the phase of the complicated part and come to a pure end," Malouf says. So Beacon was conceptualized as a high-level restaurant based around an immense, wood-burning, 700-degree stove. The restaurant is huge, with an elegant decor and atmosphere that is in no way clubby or masculine; Beacon is a serious restaurant, and looks like it. At its center is a very visible grill and oven. "We use mostly soaked apple chips for the grill," Malouf told me. "But only ash, and lots of it, in the stove. It's the stove that gives our food the wood taste. Even a lot of the things we don't cook in there [the chicken, for example, is cooked on a rotisserie] we finish in there, so it gets the taste on it too." Oddly, the items that take the smoke taste most strongly are the oysters, which become suffused by the smoke, and whose pools of water become perfumed by its woodsome essence. Other items benefit from the fact that the smoke taste does not always reach deep.

Take Beacon's sublime veal chop. A big, heavy object, it comes to you relatively unadorned on a plate. It looks like something you would hit somebody with. But once you get beyond the ragged crust and brownness of its roasted surface, the meat inside is as mild and delicate as shellfish, yet with that faint rich gaminess that is the mark of all great veal. Needless to say, the contrast between the crusty surface and the mild-white interior is an absolute jaw-dropper, particularly around the crescent edge, where fire and veal fat meet to sublime effect. Holy cow! Just thinking of it is making me hungry.

Likewise, Beacon's steaks are essays in how to serve good meat without getting in its way. The grass-fed rib eye is the best piece of grass-fed meat Mr. Cutlets has eaten, possibly as a result of its being native to these shores, and not shipped up from South America. The meat is less voluptuous than classically grain-fed American beef, particularly the fabulously rich and imperious Black Angus beef from which Beacon's sirloins are cut. But the rib eye has a kind of natural perfection to it, a be-and-let-be benevolence that is in marked contrast to the assertiveness of the sirloin. The two are like the difference between a grassy hill and the stark rugged mountains. Both have a place in Cutlets' heart, and Malouf's wood-fired grill. The rib eye is garnished with a creative chimichurri, and the sirloin features his gloss on Bordelaise. Malouf explains, "If you had sirloin in France, you would get a red wine Béarnaise sauce with it—red wine with veal stock, shallots, and black pepper. So I deconstruct that: red wine, shallots on the plate, and some black pepper, along with a little marrow." "The old 'Stockyard Delight'!" I responded. "Exactly!" Slathering soft hot marrow over this sirloin, with its woody char worthy of Mrs. O'Leary's cow, I felt an intense appreciation for Malouf's skill and devotion to historicity.

That quality is really in full effect in Beacon's annual "beefsteak" events. As described in Joe Mitchell's immortal essay "All You Can Hold For Five Bucks," beefsteaks were meat banquets held in Gilded Age New York. "Everybody gets an apron and a mug of beer," Malouf says. "Silverware is optional. We have a five-piece brass band. To start out, we send out big platters of lamb chops, double lamb chops, and then a cut of sirloin that is sort of in chunks so you can pick it up and eat it."

"Do you roll the sirloin in salt and pepper before grilling it?" I asked, thinking of Mitchell's almost-pornographic (to me) description of the traditional beefsteak.

"Yeah," Malouf replied, repressing his own drool mechanism. "It all gets season, and there is a sauce we make, basically butter, Worcestershire sauce, and pan drippings. And that gets poured all over it. A big bowl of it comes out to the table and you dip in it, and at this time everyone should have had at least four to five, to six or maybe ten beers, a couple of shots of Maker's Mark, and the band is playing and it's a lot of fun. People eat and things start getting pretty wild, actually."

I was ready to sign over my mortgage right then for the chance to attend; but in the meantime, I was glad that Beacon was open most weeknights. In spirit, if not in form, Beacon is a beefsteak every night.

Jody Speira Storch—A trip to the meat market with the proprietress of Peter Luger

Unlike the presidency, the Cy Young award, or the quality of American letters, the best steak house in New York is not a matter of dispute. Peter Luger's venerable restaurant in Williamsburg has been the ne plus ultra of red meat as far back as even Mr. Cutlets' grandfather can remember. Occasionally, enthusiastic foodies will announce the discovery of a cheaper or more conveniently located rival, which, it is always claimed, is "just as good as Peter Luger." But it never is. I had an opportunity to find out why when I visited Jody Speira Storch, one of the restaurant's owners, while she went shopping for meat on a typical weekday. (Peter Luger's is a family business, and Jody represents the third generation of the dynasty that has run it since the early 1940s.)

The Meat Market district of Manhattan, in the westmost reaches of Greenwich Village, remains sacred soil for anyone who is really serious about meat. Its wide-open brick streets and perverse past (it was where you went to pick up she-male prostitutes) have made it attractive to the beau monde, who in recent years have endowed it with art galleries, elegant restaurants, and even Alexander McQueen's new boutique. Historically, though, it is really about burly men in bloodstained white butcher coats handling carcasses on hooks. Most of the city's purveyors of wholesale meat base their operations down here, although many now operate in New Jersey or the Bronx's Hunt's Point market. But Walmir Meat Co., where I met Jody, is a particularly old-school operation. "We're one of the oldest operations in the area. We get the best whole-carcass beef and lamb from all over. We've been selling to Peter Luger since before my time, and I've been here for fifty years," one of the men told me.

Jody Speira is a handsome, youngish woman, with shoulder-length hair and a mild, easygoing manner. She could pass easily for the wife of a Ho-Ho-Kus actuary, or the principal of a progressive elementary school. You probably wouldn't expect her to be running the show at the city's most enduringly masculine restaurant, but women will be amused to learn that the template for one of New York's testosterone temples is in fact a matriarchy, its direction passed from Marsha Forsman to her daughter, Marilyn, and now to Jody.

On her regular buying trips, Jody carries with her a kind of scepter, a heavy metal die with a long handle, which she uses to mark the meat for purchase. When Jody sees a hindquarter that she finds suitable for the restaurant, she twists the die in a heavy, ink-laden brush, and whacks the meat with it, leaving a purple standard, "4 F 4." This is the family seal. It marks the very best of the best prime short loins as Luger's special preserve. The scepter itself is a hereditary artifact, its history mirroring the beginnings of the Peter Luger dynasty. Jody's grandfather, Sol Forsman, was a Williamsburg machinist who ate in Peter Luger's so often that he decided to buy it when the founder died.

Sol was the type of restaurateur, now becoming extinct, whose administration was almost Taoist in its minimalism. "Leave well enough alone" was his motto. "People complain if you make even the smallest change," Jody says. "We just stick to the way we've always done it." Sol didn't know anything about meat, however, and wisely put his wife, Marsha, in charge of that end of the business. He gave her his dye stamp, which he took with him from his machine shop across the street into the restaurant, and which Jody wields today.

"My grandmother kept shopping until she was 80," Jody muses. "She showed my mother how to look at meat, and they both showed me. It's not that complicated. You learn what to look for. There are a few basic things. First of all, it has to be prime." An old black man with a beret is swinging a whole hindquarter of a steer out of a truck and onto a meathook. (The hooks are on a long rail, and extend from the loading platform all the way to the back of the refrigerator. The hanging meat moves on them as easily as suits at a dry cleaner.) "But even a lot of the meat you see now that is labeled prime is really more like choice. My grandmother used to call it 'prime crime.' What gets called prime is a crime, you know?"

"Let's see, how big is this?" She examines a tag on the hindquarter. "760. We don't buy it if it's smaller than 800 pounds. And they grade the fat between one and five, with five being the most fatty. We like a three." The hindquarter of a steer is a big, recognizably bovine object, more like a third of a steer. Peter Luger's doesn't actually buy the whole thing, which also includes the round and other large economy cuts. Jody is there to buy the short loin, a section along the animal's spine with a large, oval "shell loin" on one side, and the small, narrow tenderloin running along the other. This area will be cut up for porterhouse steaks, such as are served at Peter Luger. A little farther down, as the tenderloin gets smaller, the steaks are called T-bones; the restaurant uses these for single portions, along with straight up shell steaks (also called strip or New York sirloin). Farther down, and of no use to Peter Luger, are the sirloin, rump, and round. Actual hindquarter carcasses look very different, I thought to myself as I followed Jody into the refrigerator, than the dotted-line diagrams you see superimposed on peaceful-looking steers in cookbook illustrations.

"We get first pick of the prime. We pay more than anyone else—that's the whole reason we have the kind of meat we do. It's not like we're putting our money into decor," she laughs. Jody named a rival restaurateur, a successful meat mogul who owns several midtown steak houses. "Our food costs are around 60 percent. That's very high. He's probably spending 30 percent on his food costs. You could find it out; it's public documentation. But a lot of the other restaurants are just buying in straight boxes."

I asked what that meant. "The meat isn't selected individually by coming down here. It comes in butchered at the source, wrapped up in plastic." Given how few prime carcasses passed muster that day, it was easy to see how a lot of lesser meat would get by were a restaurant to buy steaks en masse. This practice of essentially buying beef blind, I said, reminded me of Robert Southey's description of how sailors in Nelson's navy would eat rotten meat in the dark—"where

the eye seethe not, and the tender heart is spared."
"Exactly!" she replied.

"Now look at this one," she said, gesturing to a maroon and ochre carcass hanging before us. "I don't like the color. That's going to be trouble. We look for the color. Beautiful color is important to me. This is dark—I don't like it. You see up here, in the round? How dark that is?" Jody called one of the meat-men over, all of whom wear leather holsters out-side their white coats, containing three or four sharp knives. "Cut me off a little of this one," she asked. "Sometimes it gets a little discolored by the air, so you have to cut a little." The man offered up the meat. "No, still dark."

"Now this one is nice. You can tell from looking at the bone that it's young. You see that slight pinkness in there? The lit-tle flecks in the button? That's good. And the meat has a beautiful color, too. I'll take this one." She stamps the car-cass with the seal; it makes a heavy thwack against the meat.

"Now this one is nice, but look here," she says, pointing to a gap in the chine bone, the long, heavy ridge to which the ribs are attached. "See that space? That's trouble for me. It won't age right." She lifts up another carcass, this one with beauti-fully marbled, ruby-colored meat. This would surely get the stamp, I thought, but no. "This is callused. Go on, touch it." (It feels bumpy.) "Ropey. That's going to eat like a rock. Horrible. Prime crime," she laughs.

"These are generally Hereford cattle. There's other kinds here too, but generally I don't like them. Look at these, these are Holsteins. See how they're narrower? It's not just that they're smaller; it's going to be ropey. I want to see one that's more convex, that's nice and rounded. That's the steak that's going to give us what we want. This one has a heavy streak of fat along it; we like it to be more evenly marbled. But this is a nice one. I'll take this one."

"Your grandmother liked 'em all like that," one of the older meat-men says.

Turning to me, Jody says, "It's not a science. You just begin to get an idea of what is going to be good; you get a feeling about it. Now this one looks good—see the color? It's small, but that's OK. We can use it." Thwack. "One time we bought ten, and I stamped a couple twice. So you know what this one guy does? He cuts out the slice of fat with the stamp on it and melts it onto another hindquarter. He was trying to sell us an extra one! Then when we confronted him about it, he said, 'Oh, one of the employees did it.' Yeah, right! Like your guy is going to be so entrepreneurial? Gimme a break."

Jody finishes buying the meat for the day; all in all, she's probably picked out six or seven whole short loins. She seems pleased with the morning's purchases. She reflects on how it would eventually please the customers who would be eating it a few weeks hence. "The people who come to our restaurant know what they want. Sometimes you see them eating it, and then when it's all gone, they pick up the bone, and you're like, 'Yes!' Because then you know they really love it."

Having eaten in Peter Luger so many times, I could only nod in understanding.

5 Feature Review

Sammy's Roumanian
157 Chrystie St. | 212.673.0330

$ $ $

Meats of Note: strip steak, chopped liver

New Yorkers are generally spared the inertia that marks less competitive environments. In the outside world, a restaurant can get by for years just by being adequate, and owning its own building; here, it's an ongoing Iron Chef contest just to stay in business. Historical restaurants are an obvious exception. They are usually bad. Granted a freak immunity from the natural pressures of the marketplace, they get lazy. People are going to come there anyway, to marvel at the ancient framed images and Truman-era newspaper articles covering the walls; so why should the food be any better than it has to? Mr. Cutlets has seen this happen many times.

But the bullet has been dodged at Sammy's Roumanian, a museum diorama of New York Jewish culture as self-contained as Colonial Williamsburg. Sammy's looks more like a New Jersey banquet hall than a restaurant, a fact that is probably closer to the truth than they would like to admit.

Jews from the entire tri-state area consider it a shrine and make annual pilgrimages there for birthdays and bar mitzvahs. Set in the basement of the unhippest street on the Lower East Side, Sammy's is a square room with unframed snapshots covering the walls. Waiters are less self-consciously rude than they used to be; when I was there last, in the final days of the go-go '80s, thuggish Yeshiva boys with big hipster glasses zotzed you to the point of pogrom. Now the waiters are professional and polite, but assertive enough to let you know when you're ordering wrong. A middle-aged man at a Casio keyboard sings popular favorites ranging from "The Wind Beneath My Wings" to "Tsena Tsena," keeping up a lively klezmer beat for your entire meal. Plan on screaming if you want to be heard.

As for the food, only two items on the menu are really worth the trip. If you want to pay eight dollars for a piece of kishka (meal sausage), go ahead. Likewise, if you want a piece of Dover sole or roast chicken, it will be pretty good too. The rib steak, with its immense brown bone, makes a spectacular presentation. The veal chop is even better, particularly if you get it with garlic. But the prizes at Sammy's are the best chopped liver in the entire world, to go along with the finest skirt steak Mr. Cutlets has had the pleasure of consuming.

The chopped liver arrives in a big metal mixing bowl. Sitting in a lump at the bowl's deep bottom, it doesn't look particularly appetizing at first glance. The waiter who bears the bowl in one hand, however, is carrying two plates in the other. On one is a golden-brown pile of crisp fried onions, on the other sliced white radishes. Both go into the bowl, along with a flourished dollop of schmaltz from the syrup dispenser. A little salt and pepper and some vigorous mixing, and you're in business. A bowl of good (though seedless) rye bread is included, but the liver is better enjoyed on its own, as its soft, cold, intense flavor is delightfully cut by the crisp, cool radishes and abundant crunchy onions. In a way, the liver is condiment for the onions and radishes, rather than the other way around. In any case, it's an excellent way to ramp up to the steak. You might also want to have some cold vodka, which is poured from a bottle frozen in a block of ice. You can have them leave it at the table, but be careful, as it runs into money.

The steak, like the chopped liver, is typically Jewish—low-grade meat lovingly elevated. The menu describes it as "Roumanian tenderloin," which is a euphemism for skirt steak. Skirt steak has been rediscovered in recent years, although its intense taste and resilient texture are usually wasted on fajitas. It is a strange cut of meat—a narrow strip from the "plate" area in the steer's underside right next door to where the short ribs live. It has a grain that runs horizontally, against the cut of the narrow steak, so it's essentially pre-sliced for you, like a row of crackers, or a pile of poker chips. Sammy's has three different skirt steaks on the menu, of varying sizes, and all are immense. The medium steak hangs off both ends of the plate and comes smothered in garlic. Heady, intense, garlicky, deep pink, both tender and resilient at the same time, it comes pretty close to being the perfect steak experience. None of the side dishes are worth the time, other than the french fries, which are good and hamishe (homey).

Afterward, the waiters make an elaborate production about bringing you a carton of milk, some Fox's U-Bet, and an old-fashioned seltzer bottle to make egg creams. Keep this dubious treat for a late-night snack at home, and order the chocolate pudding, which is more in keeping with the infantile delights of Sammy's. Authenticity doesn't enter into it. Judaica is safe at Sammy's; there's no need to put it on a milk carton.

6 Keepers of the Flame

BBQ

Barbecue, the summit of the meaty sciences, is little seen in New York. Now, that isn't to say that every other restaurant doesn't promise "barbecue"; but like "Napoleon" brandy and "New York Style" pizza, "barbecue" here is merely an all-purpose marketing term. However, to those trans-Hudson peoples for whom barbecue is a culture and a calling, this language is as laughable as it is imprecise. "Barbecue," to a real pit-man, means only those meats that are cooked for long periods at slow heat, in a bath of fragrant hardwood smoke. To these men, the telltale "pink ring" is as distinctive as a papal seal, and of equal authority. Admittedly, this dogmatic stance doesn't square with our modern values, where all things are equal in the great food-court of opinion. Barbecue is whatever you want to call it, this school of thought holds. But that weighs but little with Mr. Cutlets.

The most likely etymology of barbecue is from the West Indian barbacoa, to cook meat slowly over coals. So traditional barbecue has a long and venerable history, and is subject to a vast body of erudite controversy. But, like many long-running shows in the sticks, it never made it to Broadway. The reasons were threefold. First, and most important, were the shortsighted fire regulations that prohibited the burning of long branch hardwood in an open pit. Yes, barbecue of the first class could be made in large commercial smokers, ponderous iron lungs with offset fireboxes to hold the wood. But these were so small, and required so much attention, that no commercial establishment could possibly have made money using them. And in any case, there were no first-class barbecue chefs. It takes a lifetime of sitting on a stool, drinking iced tea, learning the rhythms of slow smoke, and reading the newspaper while meat decomposes under your judicious watch. You can't teach somebody to do that at the Culinary Institute of America, and the guys that can do it live happily amid the pines of the deep south, with little thought or care for the needs of the distant and alien city. Last of all, without either pits or pit-men, there was no educated public in New York; any Bennigan's that served office workers back ribs embalmed in Kraft sauce could get the same business, for a tenth of the trouble.

The sole exception to this sad state is **Pearson's Texas Barbecue,** in Jackson Heights, Queens, an inexplicable emissary in the barbecue lands. Pearson's is real barbecue, smoked in traditional fashion over a mix of oak and hickory wood. Whatever seasonings are laid upon it are minor—like all genuine barbecue, pork and smoke are its primary elements. Pearson's' ribs are superbly understated that way. They are a bit undersmoked, and aren't desiccated enough for the meat to pull away from the bone—the point of critical mass when it comes to smoking—and they lack the lightness of depths of wood flavor you would expect from such lovingly tended meat. However, when you compare them to the sticky stuff served at high-rent joints like Soho's **Tennessee Mountain,** or **Houston's** on Park Avenue South, they're a Southern smoked treat.

Pearson's' pulled pork sandwich, unhappily, lacks the austerity that I like so much in their ribs. It's all mixed up in an abundance of sauce and served on stout Portuguese rolls. Occasionally, you see "pulled pork" that is in reality sweetened stew meat, served up out of some charlatan's kettle; but you can tell this pork was smoked into submission by the pieces of "Mr. Brown," the darkened exterior of the pork, which show up in every third sandwich or so.

Pearson's technically shouldn't be in this book, but you can get their barbecue, rushed from Queens like an organ transplant, at **Rodeo Bar,** on Third Avenue at 27th Street. The Rodeo Bar also makes excellent grilled steaks, chicken-fried steak, fajitas, and other southwestern favorites, which you can eat while listening to good country music. But going to the Rodeo Bar and not ordering barbecue is tantamount to madness. If you can eat Pearson's BBQ in an amiable room with good live music, without going to Queens, why in the name of God would you order anything else?

If Pearson's provides a glimpse of a better barbecue world, a

2001 spacepod ride is available at Virgil's on 44th Street, between Sixth Avenue and Broadway. Virgil's is a kind of meta-q, a tour through the world of low and slow such as you might expect from an eight-part documentary series on PBS. It is the greatest achievement of the late Artie Cutler, one of New York's great restaurateurs. Cutler was an entrepreneur who specialized in the annexation of whole restaurant genres: not content with his superb seafood restaurants, Dock's and Manhattan Ocean Club, he created a series of immense, elegant restaurants that took a single theme and elevated it to a new level. Carmine's, his red-sauce joint, is superb; Ollie's, his Chinese restaurant, is vast and comfortable, and as authentically good as many of the good restaurants in Chinatown, if not the best of them. Of Gabriela's, his Tex-Mex simulacra, I am unfit to judge; but I have eaten the flanken in a pot at Artie's Deli, and can declare it fit for any but the most hidebound of hungry Jews.

Virgil's is his greatest achievement, however, because in no other restaurant was the imitative challenge so great, and a successful execution so rewarding. Cutler must have said, "So they don't know about barbecue. I'll serve them the real thing, and bring the market to myself." It seems to be working. The place is always jammed—but like Ollie's and Carmine's, success was built into the plan, and so one rarely has to wait for a table. Though not a handsome restaurant, Virgil's is a museum of barbecue paraphernalia—menus from obscure pits, articles from small-town papers, signs featuring anthropomorphized pigs, the works. The educational theme continues when you sit down. The place mats feature a map of all the barbecues around the country Virgil's' creators visited and emulated in the hope of presenting New Yorkers with a fair simulation. It is like looking at a map of elephant graveyards. A dozen of the best barbecues I have ever eaten at are on it—out-of-the-way joints I assumed few northerners even knew existed, much less appreciated for the smoke-temples they are. The Pit, on the Tamiami Trail. Leo's, in Oklahoma City. Maurice's Piggy Park, in South Carolina. Even Shangri-La itself, Tuscaloosa's Dreamland, has not escaped them.

So how is the barbecue? Well, it's not in a league with any of the places on the place mat; but it is the real thing. And the one way in which Virgil's is superior to any of the barbecue-belt landmarks is in its variety. You can get obscure treats such as smoked lamb, which resembles Kentucky mutton, and comes with a mustard-and-Worcestershire sauce such as is rarely seen far from Owensboro. However, the rest of it is a mixed bag. Their pulled pork, the definitive form of the Carolinas, is better than half the ones you get at the North Carolina state fair, but there is no "Mr. Brown," and I have never liked to see a smoked meat swimming in sauce, even if it is traditional. I always preferred sliced pork, with no sauce, to pulled pork, but unhappily Virgil's doesn't go there. The brisket is too lean; I would guess that Virgil's has made the mistake of using the comparatively dry and flavorless flat cut, instead of the much richer point cut. The leg of lamb is a pallid affair when compared with the mutton it is based on, but New Yorkers still haven't come to appreciate the rank majesty of mutton just yet. As leg of lamb goes, the meat is first class, and the delicacy with which it is smoked (three hours, vs. four to five for the ribs) complements it perfectly. The sides are all superb, particularly the macaroni and cheese and the cheese grits; an appetizer or side order of bbq shrimp (really grilled) and some homemade biscuits should round out a well-balanced dinner, as they used to say in cereal commercials.

Virgil's ribs arrive with nearly 1/16 of an inch of blackened spice rub on their back—a ludicrous exaggeration of the so-called "Memphis style." In fact, all the best barbecue everywhere is dry-cooked; who is going to go into a hot pit to brush sauce on ribs while they are cooking? Memphis's barbecues tend to have a characteristic spice dust, but not the caked-on quantities as at Virgil's. However, these are thick, meaty pork spareribs whose flesh has been dyed pink by exposure to the burning wood, without ever getting dried out. They're bigger than Pearson's ribs, and so can take a longer time in the smoke.

Danny Meyer's klutzy and expensive **Blue Smoke** shows the promise of one day being a better, more imaginative Virgil's; until that day, it's a poor showing for all the talent involved, and a far cry from Meyer's other superb restaurants, like Gramercy Tavern. The problem is that Blue Smoke isn't really committed to smoking, I think—like a lot of barbecue joints, it pays too much attention to sauce, spice, and other inessentials, and as a result the barbecue tends to be hit or miss. Smoke is what makes barbecue, and there just isn't enough of it, blue or otherwise.

Don't bother with most of the other "genuine" barbecues in New York. **The Hog Pit** is designed to look like some kind of rough-and-tumble roadhouse, but that's just what it is—art direction. It's the same sweet and mushy baby-back ribs they used to serve at Tony Roma's. **Brother Jimmy's Bait Shack** is better, but still a poor showing, all around. **Brothers BBQ** presents a passable version of pulled pork, but without Mr. Brown, why bother with it at all? This was my objection in North Carolina, and it goes double in New York. If all you're going to taste is vinegar sauce, just swig from the bottle and be done with it.

As you can see, the traditional barbecue pool in New York is a shallow one indeed. But luckily, there's a wide range of places where fire and meat do mix in imaginative ways. **Beacon** represents an interesting gloss on barbecue, if only because its food is so good on its own terms, and so far from traditional pink-ring cooking. I will say that Beacon's food is much closer, in substance and spirit, to classical barbecue than the likes of Blue Smoke or Tennessee Mountain. There is just a hint of smoke about it, like perfume on a peccant husband's collar. And Beacon complements all these meats with simple but elegant sides, such as a little crock of gratin potatoes, roasted asparagus, and good sautéed spinach. And of course, as a high-end restaurant, Beacon provides an excellent, if expensive, wine list—something you don't get at Sonny Bryant's. (Of course, for me, the only thing to drink with smoked meat is orange soda—but that's just me.)

If Beacon represents a high-end version of barbecue, another vector on it can be found far downtown, at a vastly lesser cost. Technically speaking, there is no such thing as "Chinese Barbecue." The Cantonese roast meats that glint in the windows of Chinatown have never seen a flicker of fire, or a whiff of smoke. But they are intensely rich and flavorful, and valued for themselves in a way that is closer in spirit to barbecue than a lot of the stuff you see around. Take char siu, or roast pork. Char siu is the long boneless flap of meat that hangs off the end of the spareribs, roasted with a honey-based glaze, whose sweetness is tempered with spicy and salty elements like soy and hoisin sauce. The same glaze, when applied to spareribs, is even better. Ducks get their own glaze, also honey-based, but generally with a five-spice base. You also occasionally run across a flattened, tea-smoked "pu pi" duck that looks better than it tastes, though you should try it for yourself. Occasionally, as at **New York Noodletown** (Bowery at Bayard), you will also find something described as "crunchy pork," and that is something no one should avoid. It's nothing more or less than unadorned suckling pig; the crunch is unspiced, unglazed  crackling. Again, this isn't "barbecue," but given the choice between these oven-roasted meats, served in such a respectful, minimalist way, and the sauce-drenched, par-boiled debauch sold at places like Dallas BBQ, anyone who has enough sense to like real barbecue is bound to pick the former.

My favorite char siu can be found at the **Canal Fun Co.,** on Canal Street between Center and Lafayette. Unlike some of the char siu you see, Canal Fun's features a rich and rugged crust, which stands up even after it has been cut into thick slices in front of you by an elderly man with fast hands and a bloody apron. The slices, moreover, have a fair marbling of fat, and their darker, more resilient meat speaks of a more potent cut of pork than the pallid loins used by a lot of Chinese-American restaurants.

Cantonese duck is one meat Americans have rarely enjoyed: a greasy food served at room temperature, it doesn't have

much meat, and it's mostly bones. If you must get it, the best you'll find is at **Sun Say Kai,** on the corner of Walker and Bayard. The duck here is moister and softer, with a skin which, while not really crispy, at least has been rendered a little bit. Sun Say Kai's duck also has softer, less fatty skin than many Chinese ducks, and it seems to be a little more hale, though not quite plump. However, if you want to be like Mr. Cutlets, you should eat your duck submerged in soup. The fat renders in the hot broth, floating away harmlessly to become "gold coins" on the soup's surface. The broth also saturates the flesh, making it far easier to pull it away from the bone, and making life a little easier all around.

Elsewhere in Asia, other peoples have developed the "way of fire and smoke" after their own traditions. Filipino barbecue, with its vivid soy/vinegar/lemon marinades, is an absolute natural, the kind of stuff you might eat on a beach after a successful prison escape. Most inexpensive Vietnamese restaurants serve some version of thit heo nuong, or grilled pork chops. The thin chops are marinated in an appetizing mélange of sugar, garlic, and Vietnamese fish sauce, and then cooked quickly over an open fire. Because they're all surface area, every bite is stoked with marinated oomph, and the chops as a whole are crunchy and brown. Unlike char siu,

I've never had a bad Vietnamese pork chop, and the best I've had is probably at **Nha Trang** on Baxter Street, between Bayard and Canal; the **New Pasteur** next door also provides a fine rendition. Both are dirt cheap and provide a balanced meal when eaten with the fresh raw greens on the side.

As good as thit heo nuong is, though, the grilled Asian meats derby is almost certainly won by Korean barbecue, or gui. Korean barbecue is a completely different aesthetic from Chinese: there is a whole do-it-yourself aspect, for one thing, in which an elaborate table-grilling ceremony figures in. Nothing could be further from the insouciance of Cantonese noodle shops, where a guy pulls down a piece of pork, chops it into little pieces, and then pushes it onto a bowl of rice. Aside from the complexity of the process, the meat is subject to headier spices, and is set in contrapuntal contrast to a wide of variety of cold pickled treats. Koreans love the most robust cuts of beef, such as short ribs and rib-eye steak, because these stand up to their potent marinades.

Manhattan is fortunate enough to have a tight cluster of good Korean restaurants on West 32nd Street between Fifth and Sixth Avenues. All are convenient to the PATH station, the subway, and Madison Square Garden (several are also open late, making them ideal for a late dinner). 32nd

Street provides a wide range of different styles and inflections on Korean barbecue, and nearly all of them are more elegant settings than their Chinese or Vietnamese counterparts. But at the end of the day, it's all about the meat, and it's hard to pick between them, though the best of the lot, as far as I can tell, is **Kang Suh** (see page 139).

Thus ends Mr. Cutlets' survey of smoke—proof, if any were needed, that no art is alien to our island.

7 Done and Done

Ordering meat the way you want it

If there is one thing that gets in the way of the sublime pleasure of ordering and eating cooked meats, it's the communication gap between diner, server, and cook over what "rare,"

"medium rare," "medium," and "medium well" mean. (Everyone seems to know what "well done" means, since it is a terminal state, as unmistakable as rigor mortis.) The French, who take their meat far more seriously than do Americans, are in a better position, since their grades of doneness are indicated by descriptive terms: blu (cold inside), saignant (bloody), a point (almost overcooked), and bien-cuit (well done). In fact, it would be a better world if, instead of these arbitrary and subjective terms, the waiters had colored cards in their pockets, like soccer referees. Then you could send the cook a Rothko-esque floating rectangle of deep pink, the color of your gums, and that would be what came out. But as long as you have to order by standard adjectives, here are a few things to bear in mind:

- The iron laws of process control are as binding on cooks as they are on chemical engineers. You can always cook meat a little more, but reversing overcooking is only possible by starting afresh. That will take time, make you look like a jerk, and needlessly anger the cook.

- All meat continues to cook for several minutes after being removed from an active heat source. Therefore, when in doubt between two grades, order the rarer one, and let the meat sit for a minute or two, particularly in the case of hamburgers and steaks that have been exposed to searing fires.

- Giving meat a "cooling off" period, if the restaurant hasn't taken the care to do it themselves, has an added benefit as well. There is a finite amount of juice in even the richest meat; and these juices, coursing around within, will only be needlessly spilled if the meat is cut open too soon. Far better that they be reabsorbed into the meat, and released only upon contract with furiously working jaws.

- Another iron rule, applicable in every restaurant from Bennigan's to Peter Luger, may be termed the "Law of Punitive Extremes." If you get something overcooked, and send it back, you can count on it returning oozing blood; likewise, it the meat comes out as raw, and you refuse it, the subsequent version will be as dry as parched vellum. There doesn't seem to be any way around this: neither tough talk nor soft soap seem to do any good. A resigned stoicism is probably your best course.

- Although it won't help you much when you order, you will at least have a fighting chance of getting your meat the way you order it if you have an idea of what rare, medium, etc., actually mean. A trick, commonly used by chefs to test doneness without cutting, may be helpful. Touch the area directly between the base of thumb and the knuckle of the pointer finger. That's what rare feels like. The fibers of the meat haven't been heated sufficiently to start constricting. Now make a loose fist, as if you were holding a pen in it, as Bob Dole used to do: that is medium: there is still some give, but the fibers have begun to constrict, and the meat is losing its color. Now make a tight fist, of the kind needed to clean somebody's clock: that is well done. Depending on the meat, it has no more give, and no more flavor, than the average superball.

- Another point to bear in mind when thinking about how you want to order something is the presence or absence of a bone. Practically all meat is kept in a refrigerator for a long time before it's cooked. The cold gets deep into that bone; it takes a lot of cooking to get it back out. The bone becomes what physicists call a "heat sink," and the meat near it doesn't get cooked until long after the meat far from it is well on its way to cremation. Therefore, watch yourself when ordering a rib steak or veal chop rare.

- If two or more people at a table order the same thing, expect all of them to come out to the furthest degree of doneness ordered, or close to it. Forget about getting a medium-rare hamburger if the other guy orders his medium-well.

- Lastly, examine your impulses and experience before you order your meat. Why are you ordering it that way? Is it force of habit? Have you taken the cut and kind of meat into account? Have you ever tried it another way? Admittedly, these aren't the kind of experiments you are likely to try when out to dinner; but if there is some way you can conduct less pressure-packed research, it might pay off in the long run, as you find yourself enjoying your meat more, and standing a better chance of getting it the way you want it.

Ouest
2315 Broadway | 212.580.8700

💰 💰 💰 💰

Meats of Note: lamb shank, meat loaf

Ouest has a special place in New York restaurant history. The bursting of the dot-com bubble was an occasion of much bloodshed, and the shattering of many hopes; but its effect on restaurants was salutary. Once-prosperous people, their hopes of fortune dashed, chose to drown their sorrows in meat rather than jump out of windows. As the NASDAQ waned, the stock of childhood favorites rose. And no one rode the new primitivism more deftly, or more profitably, than chef Tom Valenti and his restaurant, Ouest.

Ouest might previously have seemed a long shot to define its era. Valenti was ardently admired by the comparatively small circle of gourmands who had enjoyed his work at an out-of-the-way downtown restaurant called Alison on Dominick. (Obscure, I mean, with the general public.) He had a powerful patron in Alfred Portale, of Gotham Bar and Grill. And his reputation among his peers was sky-high. But his brand of no-frills Basque cookery seemed unlikely to make waves in a city captivated, as it was then, by towering artifice, post-modern fusion cookery, and outlandish spices. That his own restaurant should finally take flight on the Upper West Side of all places, a gastronomical no-man's-land, seemed inconceivable.

But history has a way of reversing field, and the urbane razzle-dazzle that delighted the feinshmeckers of the '90s was as so much straw by 2001. New York restaurateurs found that diners were ready to leave behind the froths and chutneys that had beguiled them in the Clinton years, and embrace "comfort food": the elemental pleasures of meat and gravy, the taste of fat and infancy. "I want my food to satisfy a craving, not an intellect," Valenti has said, speaking elsewhere of the childhood "sense memories" he hoped to appeal to.

A lot of this talk is mere marketing gibberish; in fact, Valenti is an accomplished chef whose slow-cooked dishes are models of sophistication. His lamb shank, one of the most popular dishes in the city, is a good example. (Why it's available only on Mondays and Tuesdays is beyond me.) Valenti uses the fore-shank, and turns it constantly while braising, so as to draw forth maximal caramelization from the meat's ultra-succulent surface. The lamb shank is one of Heaven's gifts to trenchermen; Mr. Cutlets is always moved to offer up the most earnest orisons to the Providence that produced it. Three or four different groupings of muscle tissues run at different directions around the thick shinbone, each with a plentiful supply of fat and collagen, and each with its own taste and texture. As the shank cooks, the bone lends to these variegated tissues an intense lamby flavor, and the connective tissue holding it on disintegrates, leaving behind a velvety gelatin that binds and supports the meat like an animating spirit.

Valenti's lamb shank is enhanced by his typically understated method, invisible even to other chefs. It just appears to have fallen out of a roasting pan, with a minimum of florid garnitures. But even aside from the visual power of the shank, with its gorgeously brown surface and promise of inner vividness, there are hints of a directing intelligence behind the seeming simplicity. Take the stuff at the bottom of the deep dish; the plating is so casual, and the appearance of the big meat-bone so arresting, that you hardly notice the nubby, soupy, tan granules it rests upon. But this toasted couscous is a formidable dish in its own right—a much more rewarding variation on risotto than the grody faro or barley versions essayed by lesser cooks. The toasted couscous is primarily an absorbent starch, but it has just enough resilience to stand up to the lamb's abundant pan juices without being too grainily granular. The individual kernels are big and puffy, and after you've finished the shank, you can spoon them up along with the tiny bits of fat and flesh that remain. Hey now! The primordial bone is a Flintstone-like spectacle, and no kids need apply. But there's no denying that it is comforting— at least to Mr. Cutlets.

Other dishes on Ouest's menu, though, do leave the chef vulnerable to charges of infantile regression. Valenti is from Ithaca and has the basic hippie baggage of that city's natives—he has the long Godspell locks of so many of them, despite being nearly bald on top. (He covers the latter fact with a Hulk Hogan-style kerchief.) As a result, I think he may take his inner child a little too seriously. Ouest's beef short ribs are ably enough executed, I guess, but they don't taste like anything better than you would get in a good diner, and the soft polenta they are served upon is as bland and mushy as baby food.

These lapses are forgivable though, given the noble instincts behind them—this is a man willing to wrap Chilean sea bass in bacon. ("I'm so bad," he told New York Magazine, flying his freak flag high.) Most of Ouest's menu is just elemental enough to make people feel good, without sending them back to the crib. Even his celebrated meat loaf, which he perversely chooses to serve only one night a week, is more complex than it's made out to be, its veal-pork-beef bouquet and Worcestershire kick given smoky-sweet unction by the, yes, bacon wrapping. His roast Amish chicken and mashed potatoes is likewise masterful.

Happily, despite Ouest's commitment to the reassuring tastes of youth, the restaurant isn't very hospitable to actual children, a fact West Side diners can be thankful for. The dining rooms tend to be either up or down a flight of stairs, with the exception of the deep red leather booths that line the front of the house. It's wholly in keeping with Ouest's aesthetic that its primordial sensations, while meant to remind the aged of their youths, are in fact far beyond the grasp even of the most precocious juvenile. Only the worldliest roué, or the most jaded libertine, can appreciate "comfort food" the way it really deserves. Exhaustion, not ebullience, is the secret of Ouest's success.

9 Meat-Master Profile

The Midas touch of fried chicken virtuoso Charles Gabriel

A long-standing cooking tradition holds that a cook should be judged by the way he makes a chicken. "Poultry is for the

cook what canvas is to the painter," wrote the great gastronome Jean Anthelme Brillat-Savarin in 1825. Charles Gabriel, the founder and proprietor of Charles' Southern-Style Kitchen, on 152nd Street and Frederick Douglass Boulevard in Harlem, must by that reckoning be the best cook in town, because his fried chicken is at the very top of New York's poultry pecking order. The small buffet restaurant where his chicken is available, in unlimited quantities—along with oxtail, spare ribs, collards, yams, macaroni and cheese, and all the iced tea you can drink—doesn't look like much, but it's the foremost temple of chicken cookery in New York City. (Los Pollitos II and Alain Ducasse are the runners-up.)

The words "delicate" and "juicy" might be illustrated in future dictionaries with an image of Gabriel's chicken. His chicken is so light it could almost float off the plate, its crust is as fragile as crème brûlée. Rather than the brown and craggy, jagged crust of most commercial chicken, it is diaphanous and pale, a dully-glinting Florentine gold under the restaurant's bright fluorescent lights. The delicacy of the crust is a key, because it enhances without obscuring the meat beneath, making the chicken utterly juicy, with a toothsome, elastic give, which makes every bite an encounter. The dark meat is even better, as the spices, like the crust, amplify the flavor without getting in the way. It's a food that doesn't make itself obvious at first taste—like a girl whose beauty takes a few minutes to really appreciate.

New York doesn't really prepare you for fried chicken this good. From the candy-coated carrion served by 24-hour diners as "honey-dipped," to the wretched "Chernobyl chickens" served at places like the Port Authority, to the freakish no-skin versions served in midtown, fried chicken takes a beating in New York. Like barbecue, the lack of a discriminating public hurts its chances even more than the labor of making it the right way. Why sit around tending a burning pit, when John Q. Foodcourt is just as happy with pre-cooked ribs, sealed in sauce at the cryovac plant? And by this same logic, why go through the trouble of getting giant cast-iron pans, and keeping them going all day, when you can just dump the chicken into a deep fryer? In Harlem, though, generations of southerners have traditional notions of what chicken is really about.

Charles Gabriel was born on a farm in North Carolina. He's the acknowledged king of fried chicken among people who know a lot about fried chicken. A large man in his mid-forties, Gabriel's empire now occupies three and a half storefronts on a desolate block not far from Harlem's legendary Rucker Park basketball court. From selling chicken out of a truck, he has developed a take-out business, followed by a buffet, a breakfast place, and now a restaurant in the Bronx. The demand for his chicken drives him relentlessly forward. "I want to go downtown," he says. "Further down than here. A larger, bigger restaurant. I got a good clientele here, but the place is kind of small. You know a lot of tours, a lot of buses, have been calling me about bringing 80, 90 people, and I couldn't do it." I asked if mass production would be a problem, given the necessity of cooking the fried chicken, as he does, by hand in a cast-iron pan. "I have an idea of how—if I had a larger restaurant—I would set it up."

The cast-iron pan is the sine qua non of Mr. Gabriel's whole enterprise. Standing in front of the immense, blackened pan, he says, "This is much better than deep fried. I can get 30 pieces in there. I don't smother the chicken in the oil; I have to stand here and continue to turn it every time it gets brown. That's why pan-fried chicken is so good. It don't come out as greasy as deep-fried. That's just one reason I fry everything in the frying pan. Pork chops, too. When I opened up this business I said the one thing I would never use is a deep fryer for chicken. I only use the way my mother taught me. How are you going to open up a restaurant with only a french fry machine? So I went down south and discovered a pan. I have three of them, and they're all from North Carolina."

He gestured toward two implements, each roughly the size of a roulette wheel.

"Now, in these pans I use the pure soybean oil. Of course, country people like to use lard. But we have a lot of people here that don't eat pork. Even our collard greens use smoked turkey instead of bacon. I used to like it, but right now I can't eat lard. I don't know what it is. It don't take to me. I can't eat it. But that's all we used down south. That's all we had. But that's the only thing that's different than down south is the oil. [Lard] is what they come up eating. They feel like they at home when they come here. You know, that's why I give them the pan-fried chicken. But I only use fresh oil, and after three batches of chicken I throw it out."

As he spoke, Mr. Gabriel had set three large metal bowls on a narrow counter across from the vast, black gas range. One contained pieces of chicken, lightly spiced. The next was a mixture of milk and egg, also lightly spiced, and the third contained some white flour. As we spoke, Gabriel would pick up a single piece, briskly dip it into the egg-milk mixture, and then give it a quick flip in the flour before setting it softly into the shallow pool of hot oil. There, the chicken would begin slowly sizzling.

"Some places make the crust too crunchy. That's because they batter theirs twice, to try to get that heavy crust. That means they dip in the flour, then dip in the moisture, and then back in the flour again. I don't like that. It's one coat, and that's it. Just a nice crunchy crust, but not too much. That's why I batter only one time, in and out—that's it." Another few pieces went in. "I keep this oil at 375 degrees. That's the perfect temperature; you need it to be hot, but not too hot. It gets 175–200 back there. When it's 100 degrees outside, it's 200 in here. I'm telling you!" The pan was now half full. Mr. Gabriel turned to a nostalgic note. "Well, we had a big house, big yard, chickens everywhere. This was near Charlotte, North Carolina. We raised chickens. It was a farm. So we'd raise chickens, and eat chickens." How many chickens, I asked, would it take to feed such a big family? "Well it wasn't all of us at the same time, so we took about three chickens. There's about eight pieces to a chicken, so we'd get between twenty or thirty pieces at a time. For the whole dinner, I mean."

As Mr. Gabriel spoke, he filled the pan, and eventually the first pieces began to brown. As they did so, he gently rotated them with his tongs. After a while, they rose to the surface like gnocchi. "You know the chicken is done when it floats up in the oil," Mr. Gabriel said. When the entire pan was done, he collected the pieces into a big square metal pan with a stiff mesh rack at the bottom. He carried the pieces next door, where the buffet was beginning to run low. A large, well-dressed man whom I took for a clergyman sat at a table, neatly and purposefully working his way through a very full plate. It looked to me like he might be good for twenty or thirty pieces himself.

As I sat eating piece after piece of chicken, I wished to hear more of Mr. Gabriel's commentary, which is like an accompanying music to the chicken in my memory. What, I asked between bites, were the ideal accompaniments to fried chicken?

"Well, macaroni and cheese, that's good. But potato salad is good for fried chicken definitely—it's cold, and the fried chicken's hot, so that's very good. Potato salad and collard greens is very good. And some nice cold iced tea, that's what we serve here. Potato salad, collard greens, you got to have them—and then we got the yams and stuff alongside, but that's the main things, potato salad and collard greens." I had taken minute amounts of these dishes onto my plate, intent as I was on saving as much room as possible within me for the chicken. Now I tried contrapuntal tastes of these, especially the potato salad, which was as refreshing as kim chi. The macaroni and cheese seemed to me a waste of appetite. It was the dense, immobile kind, in which the cheese functions as mortar, and you can cut a slice as neatly as a piece of cake. Even the crust wasn't cheesy. The greens, though very tasty and impeccably light like everything else, lacked the bacony sub-foundation of the best country greens. But who cared? The chicken, in conjunction with sips of super-sweet, cold iced tea and mustardy potato salad, was all any man needed.

Eating greedily on, I asked Gabriel a question I hoped might inspire him to make a long speech I could listen to while I ate. Did he think another person, if they used the same pan, oil, spices, and everything, would make this chicken as well, without his experience? Gabriel settled back confidently; as I joyfully consumed his chicken, I was awaiting the torrent of Southern music I was sure would burst forth from him. But all he said was, "I don't think so. I don't think so." He smiled. "I'm sure a lot of people done tried."

10 Butcher Profile

Ottomanelli's Meat Market
285 Bleecker St. (bet. Seventh Ave. South & Sixth Ave.) | 212.675.4217

On the same block where Faicco's Pork Store has been churning out sausage since Theodore Roosevelt was

FRANK at OTTOMANELLI'S

president, and where Zito's has been baking bread since Frank Sinatra made teenyboppers scream (they used to ship fresh loaves to him in Palm Springs), O. Ottomanelli and Sons has been the butcher shop of choice for generations of real New Yorkers since it opened in the Depression. Today, a vestige of ancestral pride still attaches itself to Ottomanelli's. Though Old Mr. Ottomanelli has passed on, his four sons, all vigorous men in their sixties, carry on the business. Frank is in charge of beef; Jerry, game ("We call him the game warden," Frank told me); Joe is the poultry man; and Pete, the youngest, is in charge of shipping and receiving. The quality of their meats over the decades has been so dependable that their name has become synonymous with meat all over Manhattan (there seems to be as many Ottomanelli's as Original Ray's Pizzerias). Although Ottomanelli's beef, pork, lamb, and poultry are impeccable, the store specializes in game meats. "We're always on the lookout for a great thing," Frank, 70, tells me.

Frank Ottomanelli is a boyish, good-natured man with a mischievous twinkle in his eye. Having spent his entire life in the shop, he feels right at home there, and for customers, buying meat

OTTOMANELLI'S GANG

from him has the feel of visiting a beloved old uncle at his home. "All of my brothers were born in the Village, went to school in the Village, and still live in the Village," he says. Did he marry a girl from the neighborhood? "I did! We've been married for forty-one years," he says proudly. The long and stable prosperity of the Ottomanellis can be partially credited to Anthony Ottomanelli, a visionary who was one of the very first butchers to offer buffalo and bison meat to newly fat-conscious Americans in the 1970s. The old man's picture is displayed prominently on the wall directly opposite from the brightly lit meat case. He has a pensive expression. Underneath is a chair. "That's his chair," Frank says. "I always say, when he gets tired, that's where he sits down."

The store isn't very big, but it is immaculately clean, and the display case that runs the length of it is filled with a series of red and cream still lifes worthy of Matisse. Along with the familiar steaks, chops, and chickens are a number of hard-to-identify objects that look like they once walked or flew. These are Ottomanelli's' wide line of game meats—goose, quail, wild boar, you name it. "Now you take squab. A lot of people think squab is a pigeon. But it isn't—it's a non-flying bird. Maybe in the past people used to shoot pigeon and call it squab. Forty years ago people did a lot more hunting than they do today. If they shot a hare, they might have had us butcher it, and save the blood for a stew. We've sold practically every kind of game. Even brown bear—but you don't see that too often. The latest thing we got is Scotch grouse. Have you ever heard of it? They call it black cock. It's bigger than squab—with very, very dark meat. It's good though."

Frank's main concern is beef. "Beef takes a lot of care. My day begins at four in the morning, calling my suppliers. I go down to their car, see what they have. Well, we call it a car—actually, it's a trailer. But you have to go look at the meat. A lot of places don't. They just buy box meat. If they get bad steaks, there's nothing they can do about it. It's like when you buy a box of tomatoes; if there's three all wrapped up together, and one isn't as good, you're stuck with it." Frank shakes his head. "Anybody can buy box meat. It doesn't take an intelligent person. I say a three-year-old boy could do it. You have to look at the bone, feel the meat, the conformation of the carcass. But you have to get there first, and you have to pay. With the good meat you know, it's like an auction. Whoever pays top dollar gets it."

Frank often finds himself at odds with some of the city's other top butchers, such as Joe Gurrera, the owner of Citarella. "I told my supplier, Ronnie, you have to give me a break. You're giving him the cream of the crop!" Frank also finds himself bidding against the Speira family of Peter Luger fame, for whom money is no object in getting dibs on the city's best beef. But all the competition pays off: Ottomanelli's' beef is as good as can be had anywhere in the city.

I asked Frank about hangar steak, a mysterious cut that nobody on this side of the cutting table seems able to identify. In trying to ascertain its location, I also absorb some historical sidelights; Frank is a repository of butcher lore. "There's two of everything, but only one hangar steak. It's right under the diaphragm, and it holds up the kidneys. That's why it has that slight kidneyish flavor. It's the only part of the carcass that is exposed to air, and doesn't have any fat or bone covering it. So it turns dark fast. But it's very good. Butchers used to keep it for themselves. They called it 'butcher's tenderloin.' You had to ask for it specially. Now people like it a lot—it's gotten a lot more popular." Frank reaches into the case and takes out a fibrous, tongue-shaped piece of beef about the size of a textbook. It looks great. "There's a nerve running down the middle that you have to take out. You wouldn't believe how tough it is. You could probably tow a car with it, if it were long enough. Some people grind up hangar steak for hamburger; but I don't like it that way."

"You like the ground chuck better?" I ask.

"Chuck is good. Juicy. I say, if you eat it rare, you better wear a bib. But a lot of the old-timers, they come in and want a mix of neck and tenderloin. You hear that, you know they go back."

A woman standing beside me joined the conversation, and grew animated, talking about the poor quality of some ground meat she had bought out of town.

"Easy, Lisa!" Frank said, looking at her in his grandfatherly way. He sighed affectionately. "You're a good meat-eater."

"For me," Frank said, returning happily to the subject of good beef, "there's nothing like the rib. That's what my wife and I eat at home. My license plate is 'PRME RIB.' But other people like other cuts."

Another customer comes in, a heavyset Italian man wearing a suede tracksuit. At first I thought it was Vincent Pastore, The Sopranos' "Big Pussy." Instead, it was his original. "What's going on, landlord?" he asks Frank. Were Frank and his brothers landlords, I asked? "No, we're not in real estate," Frank said, chuckling at some private joke. "We'll leave that to the Trumps and Rockefellers. Meat's our life."

A pork tour of lower Manhattan

Mr. Cutlets is at a loss to explain the mysterious kinship he feels when he looks at pork. Technically, as a member of the Jewish race, there should be a vague foreboding, or at least guilt. But no! A plate of trotters sends my own feet ajumble, and a serving of sausages is to me like a ray of sunshine. Mr. Cutlets loves pork, and is sometimes even moved to squeal with delight when presented with it in an agreeable form. Meat Me in Manhattan wouldn't be complete, then, without a porkly discourse, a guide for the pig-panged. Rather than list one or another dish, though, why not accompany your corpulent old friend on a pork tour of downtown Manhattan? For that matter, why not make it a Lost Weekend-style bender? We'll go hog wild, together!

First, let's "meat" at **Beppe** (45 E. 22nd Street), a Flatiron-district Italian eatery with a three-course pork abbandonza. Beppe's "Tuscan farmhouse" cookery emphasizes beans, and the "musical fruit" is cunningly used in the first course, a grilled sausage with warm white ones. The split-grilled sausage is loosely ground and firm, with a slightly charred exterior, while the beans are falling-apart soft; together, they point up not only the sausage taste, but also its wonderfully coarse texture. In the next course, a substantial sausage ragu binds up the "Butcher's Spaghetti," giving it a densely meaty heft and taste to go along with Chianti and rosemary inflections. The Butcher's Spaghetti is all about the sausage, which is handmade from pigs raised on the chef's own upstate farm, but nothing gets in the way of the mild-salty, pungent taste. The third course, braised spareribs with tomato sauce, is as basic a pork feed as you are likely to get. The tender meat comes off the bones as easily as a stripper's spandex, and the red sauce stays out of the way. Beppe's commitment to porkery isn't all-consuming, as there are many other things on the menu, many of them quite good.

A dozen blocks or so to the south brings us to 13th Street and

First Avenue, the home of **Spanish-American Foods.** There are dozens, if not hundreds, of similar places like this around New York: tiny take-outs with a four-stool counter and one harried lady serving big portions of Hispanic home cooking. In the front window lay fat, tan empanadas; reddish-bronzed fried pork chunks; dark, spiced baked chicken quarters; and wide, tawny strips of pork rind. A big tray of sliced pernil (fresh ham) can be spied behind the counter, along with five or six well-used steam trays filled with salmon, beef stew, oxtail, pork chops, and even some stewed goat. Needless to say, Mr. Cutlets loves these places. Spanish-American Foods holds a special place in my congested heart. The fried pork chunks pack all the porky oomph of Beppe's three courses into a $2 handful of greasy-gold goodness. Fatty pieces of cheap pork, shoulder or leg by my guess, fall into the festive pop and spatter of hot oil, the elixir that, like King Midas, turns everything it touches to gold. They emerge and sit on the shelf under heat lamps, their outsides drying out while the moist meat and fat inside are cryogenically preserved. It's customary to get rice and beans with these meat confections, but I like to eat them instead as finger food with (depending on the time of day) either a diet Snapple or a quart of Old Milwaukee. They contain all a person really needs from pork, or for that matter from life; but that doesn't mean they're the only thing worth eating.

Spanish-American Foods' fresh ham is just that, fresh; shredded and juicy, it's seldom overcooked, and a portion big enough to feed three men costs only $6 and comes with equally colossal amounts of yellow rice and plump, soupy red pinto beans. The pernil sandwich, pressed flat, Cuban style, is delicious; and if you add some sun-dried tomatoes or roasted peppers from nearby Russo's, you have one of the all-time picnic classics on your hands. (And really—it will be on your hands. Bring plenty of napkins.) Every day but Wednesday, Spanish-American Foods pulls off a pork hat trick by also serving baked pork ribs in sauce, a fantastically savory dish sometimes made even better by the inclusion of beef short ribs among its riches. (And since Wednesday is Pork Chop Day at Elvie's Turo Turo [see page 136] across the street, pork fiends need not miss a beat in their daily revels.)

Spanish-American Foods is a marvel. But their stark renditions of pork are not for everybody. If you're looking for equally elemental but more sophisticated pork dishes, just walk a few blocks down by my side to **Veselka,** 144 Second Avenue. Having outed the Ukranian landmark as serving my favorite hamburger in New York, it's only fair that I do justice to its Bigos and its bacon. Described on the menu as "hunter stew," Bigos is a rib-sticking stew of pork, kielbasa, and sauerkraut, served with a heap of mashed potatoes. The kraut gives the stew a warm, vinegary undercurrent, and seeps deep into the thick, garlicky kielbasa slices and the nearly disintegrating pork. Taken together, the three ingredients meld into one, and there's almost nothing you could add to make it better. Almost. Veselka also happens to serve some of the best bacon in the city, exquisitely smoky-sweet, thick, and soft: get a side order and break it up into the Bigos. Now you're talking pork! The extra zotz of smoke, as well as the granular, toothsome contrast in texture, takes the dish to a whole new level.

By this time, your appetite may be flagging. So let us take a long and leisurely trip farther south, to a place where you'll only have to pick at a few choice morsels, while you marshal your energies for our exertions later in the evening. **New York Noodle Town,** 28 1/2 Bowery, is everyone's favorite roast-meat house. Noodle Town makes some of the best char siu (Cantonese barbecued pork) around; but its roast pork and—especially—its roast baby pork are a revelation. Many Chinese noodle shops feature what they call "roast pig," to differentiate it from char siu; but you can tell the difference just by looking. Where char siu is narrow, blackish-red, and dripping with a honey glaze, the roast pig is big and fat, and has a crunchy, peach-colored rind. Compared with its Cantonese cousin, the roast pig is bland. The tasty but tough skin and bigger pieces of meat can't hide a blah interior. But Noodle Town also serves roast baby pig, which is as tender as duck, as flavorful as char siu, with skin as light and delicious as flan. The ribs are good, too. Prefatory to the pleasure of eating Noodle Town's pork is the process of ordering it: the meats all hang appetizingly on steel rods in the restaurant's window, and you point to the one you want. A bored-looking man with a heavy cleaver pulls it down, lays it on his chopping block, and cuts it languidly apart with a few deft, quick strokes of his mighty blade. After Jack Ketch has finished his business, he slides the meat with the side of his blade onto a place with some white rice and a piece of lettuce on it.

I can see from the glow spreading on your young features that these tidbits have had their desired effect, filling you with new resolution. Excellent. Finish that Pepsi, and we'll make our way west to **Pico,** 349 Greenwich Street, for a citrus-glazed serving of roast suckling pig. Baby pig, despite its comparatively pallid taste and its unpredictability—no two portions are the same—remains the most prized of pork dishes, and in its whole form, it is surely the most spectacular. Christian Delouvier's late Lespinasse set the standard for these prestigious piglets; lesser chefs have also tried, with varying success, the hopeless project of adding, by art, a level of taste never imparted by nature. Time alone makes good pork; and time alone can supply those deficiencies that no artifice can hide. Pico gamely tries, serving a spit-roasted pig with a citrus-honey glaze. The signal difference between it and Noodle Town's is the sweetness of the skin, which doesn't add one whit to the dish, and in fact seems out of place. (A similar unease attends Maloney and Porcelli's cider-scented pork shank.) Pico is a fine restaurant, with the best sangria in New York and sublime, if undersized, interpretations of duck breast and hangar steak. But the roasted pig is a gyp, plain and simple. Luis Bello's ill-fated Meigas probably made suckling pig about as good as it can be made, at least in a restaurant. And of course a country-style whole hog feast, where you have at the carcass yourself, with your bare hands, is true pork pornography. The moral here: stick to Noodle Town for baby pig.

What's that you say? You have had enough of pig and pig talk? You are tired and full? But so many more pork temples await us further downtown! We haven't even got to our first barbecue yet. Bah! I had hoped to find in you a disciple, an acolyte to carry forward the love of pork to the twenty-first century. Be off, then! Mr. Cutlets will corner the market on pork futures, as he has pork pasts. Swine is mine.

Faicco's Pork Store

260 Bleecker St. (bet. Sixth & Seventh Aves.) | 212.243.1974

People who like sausage, the saying goes, would do well not to watch it being made. Yeah, right! That nostrum was refut

ed once and for all when Mr. Cutlets visited Faicco's Pork Store, on Bleecker Street. Faicco's is a meat-culture institution, a touchstone for Italian-Americans all over New York and New Jersey. The whole block, in fact, is a kind of Ellis Island museum, in which the assimilated see how far they have fallen from the true way. Next door to the celebrated sausage maker is John's Pizza, an institution in its own right; down across the street is the equally famous Murray's cheese shop, and a few hundred feet to the west the Ottomanelli brothers embody the best of the old-time butcher shop. The legendary Zito's bakery, Sinatra's favorite, is also across the street. If I could live on any one block in Manhattan for eating purposes, it would be this one.

As for the sausage-making process: Faicco's has absolutely nothing to hide. It is a brightly lit, clean store with a big refrigerator case running along its length. It carries a full line of salamis, cheeses, and fresh meats, but the star attractions are a variety of freshly made sausages. "People like that you can see it getting made," Eddie Faicco tells me. "Some other places cut corners. Not us."

Eddie is a serious-looking young man who, at 34, has inherited the business, and tends to it with earnest dedication. He oversees every aspect of the sausage-making process, from buying the pork butts and the natural casings, to grinding, spicing, and finally, forming the sausages.

Faicco's sausage-making process couldn't be simpler: Eddie or one of his guys grinds the sausage in an immense, ancient machine, which sits at the rear of the place, just beyond the refrigerator case. "This is so old, that we couldn't even get it fixed if it ever broke. We can get new belts for it, but that's it." A relic from the golden age of heavy industry, this massive engine grinds hundreds of pounds of pork each week within its massive gears. A broad, spatula-like piston mixes the ground sausage with some water and a few cups of the house salt-and-pepper mixture, and possibly a little fennel or red pepper flake, depending on what's being made. That's the whole sum of ingredients in Faicco's sausage. But the difference is really noticeable—it's softer and fuller, less grainy than most of the Italian sausage I've had, and more packed with porcine goodness. Faicco's supplies some of the best red-sauce restaurants in the city, such as Carmine's, F.illi Ponte, D'Annico's, and of course John's Pizza next door.

As Eddie goes through the familiar task of grinding the sausage, he underscores again for me the difference between Faicco's and lesser sausage makers. Faicco's sausages are made entirely from fresh pork butts (shoulders). The butt has plenty of fat, and its toughness derives from the multiple muscle groups running in different directions around the joint. Once ground, though, shoulder tends to make the best and juiciest meat—just as with beef, where ground chuck is the hamburger cut par excellence. "Good ingredients, good product. You charge what you have to. Our customers don't mind." Occasionally, a customer will qualm at the relatively high price. Eddie regards these misguided souls with pity. "Some people don't know any better," he says. "I was brought up around food, so it's easy for me to know that. But some people don't. If they want to buy sausage in the supermarket, hey! Go ahead. They don't know what they're getting."

"Some places use scraps. Or they'll add nitrates. You buy it and it looks fresh, but when was it made? It might have been two weeks ago. Or they'll add fat in to make it bigger, but then it shrinks down when you cook it." As he speaks, Eddie is taking down a long, translucent ribbon that resembles nothing so much as an endless condom. He runs some water through it, and then finds the beginning, fixing it to the long, tubular extremity of another machine, this one mounted on a broad and spotless steel table. The machine has a cone to feed meat into, and the narrow tube sticks out of the side. It is to this tube that Eddie now slides the full length of the casing, pushing what look like yards all into a few inches of the pipe. "We don't sell anything here that we wouldn't serve at our own house. I grew up eating this sausage in the Sunday gravy. You know what I mean? I have to say, too, that when you make a good product you get quality people coming in. They want good stuff, and we see them every week. When it's slow, that's when I go crazy. I like the pressure."

The machine is now humming, extruding a steady stream of sausage into the casing. Eddie lets out the material a little at a time, until a single sausage three or four yards long rests on the table. He twists off eight-inch sections, which magically now look like the familiar sausages, ready to be cut apart, or stolen by a mischievous mutt, who will run away with a string of them in his mouth, as in old cartoons. (Or they may also be used to lure away a menacing-looking watchdog.)

Sausages aren't the only thing to go to Faicco's for: its Italian meats and cheeses, such as salami, braciole, pancetta, and fresh mozzarella, are all out of this world. More special still are the prepared specialties, such as the prosciutto bread, a soft, moist, densely chewy roll studded with thousands of tiny cubes of the salty cured pork. The pizza rustica, a heavy, coarse quiche jam-packed with Italian hams, is even better.

Faicco's has come a long way since its founding in 1900; a large picture hanging on the back wall shows the place on a grim day in the 1930s: sawdust covers the floor, and four melancholy men stand around facing the camera. One holds a knife. Eddie could easily fit into that picture, it seems to me. He seems a throwback to his ancestors, with his solemn style and jealous devotion to sausage excellence. That the place is now immaculately clean and brilliantly lit takes away not one whit from its old-school ambience, or the people responsible for it. The place is packed full of the past: At Faicco's, history is ground out every day.

While Eddie makes the sausage, a dozen people have come in. "You have to excuse me," he says. "Everybody's coming in for meat for the Sunday gravy." He goes over to a friendly-looking lady in her sixties. "Can I get four pounds of the sweet?" she asks.

13 The Beef Less Eaten

Beef you don't see every day

Everybody loves meat. And of all meats, meat-lovers seem to prize beef best. And why not? The taste is transporting, complex, and rich. Nothing is more substantial; nothing complements so many different sauces and spices; and nothing needs sauces and spices less. It's so good that chefs are best advised to just get out of its way. But if New York's chefs haven't been able to improve on beef cookery, they've been exploring and exploiting different kinds of beef all the time. A handful of cuts—"New York" strip steaks, tenderloins, rib eye or "Delmonico" steaks, and prime rib—used to serve most restaurants. Post-modern meat-eaters, though, now find themselves face-to-face with parts of the steer that they didn't even know existed. Is oxtail really . . . oxtail? Is there a difference between short ribs and flanken? And just what is hangar steak, anyway?

Here are five less-well-known cuts of beef, as they are served, at their best, in one of New York's beef baronies. All five cuts come from parts of the animal that were once thought unworthy, such as the chuck (shoulder) or short plate and flank (underside). But now we know better, and the world is a better place for our knowledge.

Hangar Steak > Les Halles
411 Park Ave. South (bet. 28th & 29th Sts.) | 212.679.4111

Hangar steak is one of those cuts of meat so obscure that only butchers used to know about it. A smallish muscle beneath the diaphragm and above the kidney, it's earthy and intense, vividly juicy, and tender too. It's so good that butchers used to keep it for themselves. (If you wanted it, you had to ask for a "butcher's filet," and hope your meat man liked you.) The hangar steak, or onglet, has a succulent, robust character that you seldom find in even the best strip steaks. But don't order it well done—overcooked, it becomes bitter, and as tough as whitleather. For all its admirable qualities, hangar steak is still an economy cut; the sushi-size portions doled out by some of these downtown "wanna-bistros" amount to highway robbery.

For a terrific hangar steak, go to Les Halles, Anthony Bourdain's commendably meat-centric restaurant on Park Avenue South. "Hangar steak is much more interesting to me than filet mignon," opines Bourdain, the author of Kitchen Confidential. "It has a slightly ropy texture, and a stronger flavor that I love." The onglet arrives, grilled precisely to order, and served with a savory but unnecessary wine and shallot sauce. Les Halles isn't cheap, but the cost doesn't seem excessive once you cut through that sizzling surface and see why the butchers kept it as their private preserve.

Short Ribs > Balthazar
80 Spring St. (east of Broadway) I 212.965.1414

Flanken in the Pot at Artie's Deli > Artie's Deli
2290 Broadway (at 83rd St.) I 212.579.5958

New York's last big beef innovation—and one whose reverberations are still being felt in gall bladders all over town—was the rediscovery, in the wake of the dot-com boom, of so-called "comfort foods." Chief among these were short ribs, whose dense, fibrous, and fatty meat is broken down by long, slow cooking, and becomes as tender and reassuring as a crisis counselor. Of course, short ribs are so popular that you can get them spiced and prepared every imaginable way. Dan Silverman, during his tenure at Alison on Dominick, even made a little short-rib terrine—a kind of meat mousse. Still, the classic mode of preparing short ribs, oven braising with aromatic vegetables and red wine, is the best and most spectacular, which is why **Balthazar** serves it as their Saturday night special. It's easy to get distracted by all the supermodels in Keith McNally's celebrated eatery, but these ribs are magnificent, particularly with a bottle of Cotes du Rhone and a plate of crispy french fries.

Flanken, short ribs' homey kosher cousin, are also good, but they're not the kind of thing you would want to order in a good restaurant. They're tough and basically unambitious: all they want is to be boiled at home in plain broth and served to some beleaguered loved one. **Artie's Deli,** on the Upper West Side, takes the extra step of finishing them in mushroom barley soup, which provides a velvety backdrop, and also absorbs a soft, deep beef undercurrent itself. Flanken has even more collagen, or connective tissue, than short ribs do, and is fattier too, so when it cooks down it releases much fluid into the thirsty barley. It's a great dish for a cold day, empty pockets, or a depressed spirit.

Oxtail > Five Points
31 Great Jones St. | 212.253.5700

It doesn't take a genius to figure out where oxtail comes from. The name isn't at all poetic. It really is tail meat. It's from a steer rather than an ox, though. (Oxen pull things around, and are only eaten when times get tough. Steers, on the other hand, are beef cattle neutered before impure thoughts can spoil their taste.) Oxtail is a delicacy, extremely rich and delectable, that is found most often in Caribbean and soul food restaurants. An upscale version, however, can be had at Five Points, and makes an ideal introduction to this peasant treat. Five Points, an elegant restaurant in an especially stylish Noho neighborhood, seems an unlikely place to get such poor man's fare. But Five Points is at its best with hearty dishes (their pork chop is all-world) and they serve a refined, artistic oxtail appetizer, plated on a petite, oblong dish with its own braising sauce and a wood oven-finished poached egg. You break the egg, and the bright taste and color of the yolk contrasts beautifully with the dark brown of the melting meat. I'm not saying you should get it as a prelude to Five Points' stellar rib steak. But Mr. Cutlets would be behind you 100 percent if you did.

Skirt Steak > Churrascaria Plataforma

316 W. 49th St. (bet. Eighth & Ninth Aves.) | 212.245.0505

In a way, it's crazy to go to Churrascaria Plataforma for any particular dish: by the time you've been there fifteen minutes, you can hardly tell one kind of meat from another. Like all riodizios, the place has a tomorrow-we-die format, featuring an army of waiters circling the restaurant carrying skewers of grilled, marinated meat. Of those 18 different kinds of meat, though, the churrasco, or skirt steak, is chief. (The restaurant is named for it, after all.) You may have encountered skirt steak in one of its other guises—as sizzling ribbons of fajita meat, for example, or as a garlic-laden "Roumanian tenderloin" at old-time restaurants like Sammy's, on Chrystie Street. But churrasco is Mr. Cutlets' favorite form of skirt steak. Skirt is long and narrow, fibrous meat, with a horizontal grain that makes it easy to cut; and like hangar steak, it has a depth of beefy taste that can be life-altering. Grilled on a hot fire and served medium rare, garnished with a dollop of garlic, parsley, and onion chimichurri, and cut by a sharp knife, this is as good as skirt steak gets. It's especially good when taken with one or more caprihinas, which go down almost as easily as the meat.

Peter Luger Steak House

178 Broadway, Brooklyn I 718.387.7400

Meats of Note: porterhouse steak

Some measure of the thrall that Peter Luger has cast over New York's meat-eaters can be found by eating in other steak houses. Generally, all strive to emulate Luger, genuflecting to all the external forms of the Luger experience—the sliced porterhouse served on an inclined platter, with a pool of savory fat at the bottom; the gruff waiters; the perfunctory appetizers. Unhappily, none of these things is essential to Peter Luger's real appeal, which lies entirely in the quality of its meat. That meat—hand-selected by Marilyn or Jody Speira, dry-aged for weeks, and broiled under infernal flames—is the ne plus ultra of steak in New York City. Period. These steaks have a mineral sharpness, a vividness of flavor that shows up its rivals for the marketing exercises they are.

The Peter Luger steak is so good that the waiters actively discourage the ordering of anything else—a hard business anyway, since the only other things on the menu are double-cut lamb chops, also superb, and a pointedly bland salmon. (What is someone doing at Peter Luger who doesn't want meat?) The meal generally begins with a basket of crusty caraway seed rolls, whose unexpected excellence has ruined many a meal by sating what should be a ferocious appetite. That's why the appetizers are so minimalistic—a slice of onion and tomato presents no bulk, and so detracts little from the main business of the evening. Serious meat people would do well to order the thick sliced bacon, which is hammy, fairly lean, and served plain. (Few people today have the constitution to order the lamb chops as their appetizer, as Mr. Cutlets' sainted father used to.)

The historical roots of the Luger meal lay in the old-time "beefsteaks" thrown in the gilded age, when gluttony was frankly embraced as the order of the day. As described most memorably in Joseph Mitchell's essay "All You Can Hold For Five Bucks," these meals were awe-inspiring catered events, at which endless plates of broiled, sliced-up shell steaks were accompanied by equally endless pitchers of cold beer. Before the steaks, the diners were fed lamb chops, beef kidneys, and hamburgers made of the ground tails and trimmings from the steaks. Then would come the steaks, broiled, sliced, and served on toast. The meat was rolled in coarse salt and pepper, which created a crust to hold the juice in. But once cut, that hot blood and grease would course downward into a bowl, where it was then mixed with butter and Worcestershire sauce, and spooned back over the sliced steak. The result was something very like an orgy, to hear people tell it. "In the old days," one beefsteak functionary told Mitchell, "they didn't even use tables and chairs. They sat on beer crates and ate off the tops of beer barrels. You'd be surprised how much fun that was. Somehow it made old men feel young again. And they'd drink beer out of cans, or growlers. Those beefsteaks were run in halls or the cellars or back rooms of big saloons. There was always sawdust on the floor. . . . The men ate with their fingers. They never served potatoes in those days. Too filling. They take up room that rightfully belongs to beef and beer."

The beefsteaks were occasions for great, Dionysian revelry, and were marked by a spirit of abandon. Although since domesticated by effete innovations such as silverware, the spirit (and more importantly, the flavor) of the beefsteak is still alive at Peter Luger. The prevalent feeling you get when you are there is euphoria. Everyone seems glad to be there and to be alive; everyone lets themselves go. The Spartan plainness of the place, its scuffed floors and beat-up benches, helps to put you at ease, to say nothing of the huge drinks you're served as you wait for your table. But the main engine of Luger's euphoric effect is the meat. Meat has only gotten worse in the hundred years separating the beefsteak era from our own; but Luger's is one of the few places where the meat is probably pretty much the same as was eaten by the beefsteak eaters of Mitchell's day.

Peter Luger's serves only porterhouse steaks, which are sometimes mistakenly called T-bones. (The T-bone is really just a junior porterhouse.) The porterhouse is the noblest of all steaks, since it miraculously provides, on one bone, two entirely different kinds of steak—both of which are generally agreed to be the very best of their kind. For people who value tenderness most in a steak, and whose greatest praise is "you can cut it with a fork," there is the tenderloin; for those who value flavor and a fine-grained but well-marbled fullness, there is the shell loin or New York strip. It's easy to take a slice of each as soon as the steak arrives, and when surrounded by a constellation of crusty hash browns, creamed spinach, and ample spoonings of the blood, butter, and Worcestershire gathered at one end of the platter, you can see how it makes people so giddy. (It wouldn't kill you to spoon a little of the juice on your hash browns, either.)

The service at Peter Luger, which is invariably provided by middle-aged German waiters, tends to be a bit brusque; they know how you should order better than you do, and have neither the time nor the patience to pretend otherwise. Beepers on their hips are constantly summoning them to pick up steak, and there's no decision to make anyway. You get your steak very fast, and it's almost always done as ordered. (The plate is so hot, though, that should a few slices be too rare, you can leave them to sizzle against it.) Afterward, try to free up a few centimeters of intestinal space for the chocolate mousse cake, with a heavy dollop of shlag (fresh whipped cream) on top. Some people have a glass of strong, fresh Martin Bros. coffee afterward. Save the bone for a Proustian flashback later, when you have come down from the high. Standing meditatively at the refrigerator, amidst the solitude and silence of your own home, you will remember the fellowship of the beefsteak-eaters—and wish you were back there. And, as with so much else in the world, all it takes is a fat stack of cash. Peter Luger doesn't accept credit cards.

15 Augers and Omens

How to tell a good restaurant
without actually eating there

Mr. Cutlets is a kindly and conscientious guide. He will not steer you far wrong. Avuncular and corpulent, a friend to adventurous youth and a companion to sated age, he will always do his best to guarantee a good meal for you and your loved ones. But this manual doesn't pretend to be comprehensive, and a reader may well find him/herself at the threshold of a place not vouched for by Mr. Cutlets. At that point, these few guidelines may help to maximize your chance of getting the good meal you so richly deserve. Here are several things you can look for in a restaurant, anywhere in the world, even without going in:

- At one time, it was believed by trenchermen that a chef should be fat, and that the presence of a thin man behind the stove was a portent of disaster. Alas, this is no longer the case, and the number of fine young chefs makes it irrelevant anyhow. (Even the most appealingly obese restaurateur was young and thin once.) This having been said, a merry fat man is always a good sign.

- What non-culinary assets does the restaurant have? Generally, the laws of thermodynamics apply to restaurants, and none more so than the law of conservation of energy. Few restaurants are any better than they have to be, and if a restaurant has a peerless location, historical distinction, live music, plenty of models eating there, or an exquisite design scheme, these should all be counted as demerits unless you hear otherwise. This is always true, but particularly when outside a competitive restaurant environment like New York's.

- Don't be snobby about franchise restaurants; some are pretty good, and all are consistent. A disoriented gourmand, lost in a strange city, could do much worse than eating at Morton's, Ruth's Chris, or even the likes of the Outback Steakhouse. Opinion varies on all of these, but once you have identified one you like, remember: even if it isn't that great, it is a sure bet, and nothing is more precious than that.

- The most important measure of any restaurant, other than the food itself, is the menu. Happily, you can usually read this from the outside. If not, it isn't impolite to ask the captain or server for a menu to look at.

- Generally, try to look for places in which unusual cuts are served. A restaurant whose only beef dish is a strip steak, or whose only chicken is a breast, is only serving meat because they have to. Whereas the man who puts hangar steak, skirt steak, sweetbreads, or pork bellies on a good menu is the man you want working for you. But meat in and of itself doesn't tell you much. A restaurant may do the same pedestrian work on guinea hen or venison as a Pennsylvania roadhouse's "Hamburg Steak."

- Likewise, keep an eye out for evidence of restraint and minimalism. Since the advent, in recent decades, of menus that tell you every ingredient in every dish, there's been a temptation constantly present to try to beguile customers with exotic ingredients, strange spices, and ostentatious platings. There are very few chefs that can bring this kind of thing off. Jean-George Vongerichten can mix lamb with seven spices and cucumber mint relish; you don't know the same about the man or woman whose restaurant you are about to entrust yourself to. Generally, fewer ingredients, less flash, and a willingness to let meat flavors rule themselves are good signs.

- If it looks like a hundred other menus, that's not a good sign: a guy who opens an Italian restaurant only to serve veal piccata and pasta primavera either doesn't have his heart in it, or is completely unimaginative. Either way, it's a red flag.

- Likewise, avoid any restaurants whose menus are laser-printed in cursive script. Zany fonts, whimsical names for the dishes, or jocular descriptions are likewise bad omens. Good cooking is serious business.

- Don't eat in any restaurant whose menu says "Bill of Fare" at the top.

These tips may not in themselves suffice to find Mr. Cutlets' reader the nourishing meal s/he needs, but at the very least, it should provide something to go on. The perturbations of a troubled conscience are not easily stilled, once they set in. Mr. Cutlets second-guesses himself for weeks after a bad restaurant decision. Sure bets have ever been my motto; every bad dinner is an irrecoverable error, which can neither be blotted out from memory, nor redeemed by remorse. Bend your mind, and play the percentages: fortune favors the cautious, in eating as in everything else.

16 Meat-Master Profile

Sandy Levine, MBD—
Behind the scenes with the
manager of the Carnegie Deli

The Carnegie Deli, as a citadel of Jewish food, is as eminent in its own sphere as the concert hall a block away from which it derives its name. Nearly everybody has heard of the place, and despite the sky-high prices and touristy atmosphere (the gimmicky menu features dishes with names like "The Egg and Oy" and "Nosh, Nosh, Nanette"), it lives up to the billing. If you're here from Oklahoma, and want to find out what a pastrami sandwich is, this is the place for you to go. It therefore occupies the same place for New York as does, say, the Commander's Palace in New Orleans, or Pat's Steaks in Philadelphia: it's the place where the city's signature food is most famously served.

This might seem like a broad claim to make. But it really isn't. New York is the most cosmopolitan restaurant city in the world, proverbially "transnational." But still, how many foods are primarily associated with New York alone? The New York strip steak grows on cows in every clime. Pizza entered America via New York, but has become completely naturalized. You could make a good case for the "New American" movement being associated with New York chefs like Larry Forgione and Alfred Portale, but Alice Waters in Berkeley was the original innovator. Global fusion cooking, though represented here to best effect in places like Nobu and Vong, by definition has no home. So that leaves the Jewish-American glosses on east European kosher cooking that people ate here while the rest of America knew only waffles and hamsteaks. None of the dishes are native: pastrami is Roumanian, bagels Polish, and corned beef British. Our only gastronomical innovation as a people was probably the fountain sodas of which the only survivor is the egg cream. But no other place but New York ever really picked these up. That leaves the great deli standards, of which pastrami is the hardest to emulate, and arguably, the best. If the ultimate New York meat is a New York pastrami sandwich, the paragon of pastrami in New York is the Carnegie Deli.

That's a serious responsibility, but Sanford Levine, MBD, the Carnegie's manager, doesn't seem to take it too seriously. A bald, genial man with a commanding manner, Sandy enjoys talking about his business; he has the zeal of the convert, having taken control of the restaurant a mere ten years ago, when it was already an institution. "Do you know what MBD is for?" he asks impatiently. "Married boss's daughter!" Sandy married Marian Parker, the daughter of Leonard Parker, the restaurant's founder. Parker is an elderly man, who is often pictured holding a pickle nearly his own size in the place's promotional materials. (Even in the picture, which is years old, Parker looks tiny and wizened, a Yoda. You wonder how big that pickle really is.)

Sandy's stewardship of the famous deli has been conscientious. "We fine-tune a little here or there. We added a turkey burger. But we didn't go crazy. People know they can come here to get the best. What makes us different? We do all our own processing. We have complete control of the whole process; we don't buy from jobbers. Anyone can throw a corned beef in a pot. We cure ours for 14 days. Our pastrami is cured and smoked at our own place in New Jersey. And everyone who works here has been brought along slowly, and taught exactly how to do everything." Sandy stopped a passing staffer, a Hispanic man in his late 20s.

"What did you do here when you started?" Sandy asks him.

"Dishwashing."

"Good. Good-bye," he says, continuing. "Everybody here starts as a dishwasher. By the time they move to wait staff, or behind the counter, they've been here a while, and we know them. They learn exactly how we like things done."

Another man is walking by. "Ricky, how many years have you been with us?"

"Twenty-three years."

"How did you start?"

"Dishwasher."

"Ricky's been with us for twenty-three years. This is how we get the kind of consistency we are known for."

Sandy is as proud of the food itself as he is of the staff. "I eat a few sandwiches a week. You can't eat it every day. But we have a lot besides the sandwiches. A lot of our older customers still eat the traditional dishes. Chicken in a pot is still a best-seller. We have flanken, goulash, and a lot of the older people eat a lot of that. Kishka. You see we still serve Cel-Ray tonic. [Cel-Ray is a celery-flavored soda, a relic of the old days when people liked bad things.] Not many people still order it. But we have it. Shirley—how many Cel-Rays we sell today?"

"None."

"That's what I mean. But we still keep it. Most people don't know about Cel-Ray. Do you drink it?" I said I didn't. "That's for the real old-timers. But we take care of everybody." Sandy leaned over to the next table, where a perplexed-looking man was trying to eat a gigantic Reuben sandwich. "Where are you from, sir?"

"Austin, Texas."

"See?" To the man, he said, "Why did you come here?"

"I had read about corned beef and I wanted to try it."

Sandy's face took on a beatific expression. "Well thank you, sir. I hope you enjoy your meal."

He turned to me. "See, he knew where to come." (Sandy said nothing of the fact that the man was experiencing corned beef in its most degraded form, smothered under Swiss cheese and sauerkraut. The Carnegie hides the Reuben sandwich, the invention of a cross-town rival, at the bottom of its menu; as a purist, I was sure Sandy must loathe it.) "Today, we have a lot of competition. 16,000 restaurants. There's fusion, Asian, Thai, sushi. People eat Tex-Mex food— they want fajitas, chuhitas, chalupas, who knows. But we serve them the genuine deli food." Sandy reflected on his good fortune. "I love it. Other people get excited hitting a golf ball, or hitting a tennis ball. To me," he gestured around at the bustling restaurant, "this is more gratifying."

Carnegie Deli
854 Seventh Ave. | 212.757.2245

Meats of Note: pastrami, corned beef, brisket

The Carnegie Deli, to a practiced eye, doesn't look like it should be a definitive New York food institution. It's flashy and self-promotional, a magnet for free-spending tourists who don't know bupkis, and its über-Jewish authority would seem to be belied by the fact that nearly everyone who works there is Hispanic. It's also astronomically expensive. But none of that matters. The food at the Carnegie Deli is superb, consistent, and absolutely genuine. It's the federal reserve of deli food. You can take it to the bank. Now, this isn't to say that the Carnegie is better than Katz's, Wolfie's, and other, equally venerable delis. But the Carnegie is the place every-body knows best, and it always delivers.

Take the pastrami sandwich. Like all of the Carnegie's sand-wiches, this is a monstrosity—six inches tall, with over a pound of hot, thinly sliced, meltingly fatty and peppery pastra-mi squeezed between two thin slices of seeded rye. The bread is so insufficient to this load that the meat's perspiration, naturally discharging into it, turns it to mush. (The Carnegie will supply you with extra bread at a surcharge. The cost is justified, though, as there is more than enough meat for two men—or four Scotchmen, as the regulars might say.) The Carnegie, encouraged by the awe of tourists, has set upon the project of overbuilding sandwiches with what amounts to a postmodern zeal. There are double sandwiches, a foot high with three kinds of meat, and grotesque compounds of meat, cheese, chopped liver, whole wedges of lettuce, whole tomatoes, and worse. Needless to say, these things should only be understood as conceptual art, and should never be ordered, or even seen for that matter. Your time would be better spent contemplating the vast collage of signed celebrity headshots covering nearly every inch of the Carnegie's walls. New b-list stars are rotated out periodically, but you can still find pictures of Friar's Club sachems like London Lee, Corbin Monica, and of course Danny Rose himself.

Essentially your choice boils down, as it were, to three kinds of boiled brisket. (Technically, pastrami is made from navel, but few people can tell the difference.) Pastrami is a cured meat, with a peppery exterior and a piquant flavor; corned beef is similarly cured, but in a much milder, saltier brine, and without the thick, dry spice rub; and brisket is uncured and unseasoned, simultaneously minimalist and voluptuous. All three are great. The other sandwiches are well made, but by no means worth the money, with the possible exception of tongue, which I'm not qualified to judge. In any case, all three sandwiches are yieldingly tender and succulent. As Carnegie founder Leonard Parker once said of his hot sandwiches, "If you have to chew it, you might as well eat gum." Atkins dieters can get either the pastrami or the corned beef as hash, with or without an egg.

A shiny metal bowl of pickles will keep you occupied while you look at the vast menu. It includes everything under the sun, but as with the sandwich section, your real choices are in fact much smaller. The matzoh ball soup is refined and intense, but too filling if you plan on eating anything else; even if you don't eat the softball-size meal cake, it will take the edge off your hunger, humans having when all is said and done a finite capacity for animal fats. The other choices come down to broiled flanken, chicken in a pot, garlic chicken, pot roast, and chicken paprikash. All of these are classic renditions, as historically accurate as a butter churn in Colonial Williamsburg. The menu's other standouts, evanescent blintzes and outstanding lox and eggs, are not properly the subject of this manual, but I will vouch for them anyway.

Dessert at the Carnegie Deli generally takes the form of one of the immense cakes that rotate, like circus elephants holding each other's tails, in a refrigerated display case next to the cash register. The most famous of these is the cheesecake, which the Carnegie sells as a gift item in a special box. It really is superb. It's as heavy as depleted uranium, with an unmistakably creamy foundation and a perfect cookie dough crust. Sometimes I will get a piece of black and white chocolate mousse cake, but if you have room for even a little bit of dessert, you clearly haven't done your job here.

A fable

There were at one time, in this city, seven brothers, each of whom sought to surpass the others in the arts of gulosity. From their respective apartments around the city, each brother set out, with the unwholesome vigor of the libertine, to leave such a mark on his neighborhood as might ever afterward rebuke lesser constitutions.

The first brother specialized in sausages; wursts were his passion, and the thought of headcheese sent him into raptures. Shaller and Weber, on East 86th Street, was an earthly paradise to him, and seldom a day arose when he did not wake to thoughts of it.

Brother Two enjoyed sausages as much as the next man, but only in the greater context of breakfast meats. Bacon, ham, pork roll, and scrapple were as ambrosia to him, and exotic dishes such as souse and pudd'n cookie well nigh psychedelic. His mecca was Union Square Market, where good-hearted hippies and stern Amish dealt in the stuff of his ardor.

The third brother loved squid, from beak to point, and savored the taste of a tentacle. At Hop Kee, on Mott Street in Chinatown, he ate salt-baked squid to his heart's content, and found in the practice of scoring the edges for extra crispness a proof of Oriental sublimity.

The passion of the fourth brother was french fries, and Katz's Delicatessen the object of his fetish. There, on platters too hot to touch, thick, oil-logged, starchy fries were to him an image of the good life, and he frequently got them to go.

The fifth brother was devoted to pork chops. No other cut of meat could satisfy him, and his greatest joy was the sight of two bronzed and arching chuletas, bounded by a golden crescent of fat. La Dinastia, at 145 W. 72nd Street, met his exacting requirements with eminent consistency, and in return enjoyed his patronage on an almost daily basis.

The sixth and seventh brothers were attached to pork ribs

and short ribs, respectively. While six would wade into a platter of spareribs at Virgil's, his brother would be gratifying his longings with Artie's flanken in a pot. Each was happy with his lot, and neither wished for anything better under the sun than to have one more rib to nibble, with one more in reserve.

Such were the dispositions of the seven brothers, and they might have continued in their happy rivalry to the present day, had they not fallen prey to the greatest weakness of the gourmand. I refer to the opiate fumes of curiosity. Where there is much to be enjoyed, the grasping spirit supposes there is little to be lost by venturing outward; where there are calm waters and a green pasture, the well-tended lamb thinks himself a sea serpent, or forest predator, and longs for the habitat that will destroy him.

After much boasting, and long nights spent in crafty wiles, each of the brothers determined to annex the others' demense. The fifth brother, lured to Mott Street by his brother's hectoring, was seduced by Hop Kee's superb Peking Pork Chops, and was lost to his home kitchen forever. He seldom enjoyed La Dinastia with his old simplicity, and found himself always longing for the sweetness of Hop Kee.

Brother four, the imp of inquisitiveness now firmly planted in his mind, in turn visited La Dinastia, and found its thin, crisp, wonderfully fresh french fries such a novelty that he was never again able to feel completely comfortable in Katz's. Brother one then began buying Green Market sausage, while brother seven presumed to try the flanken-inflected meat ragu at Carmine's, and brother two found the selection of breakfast meats at Shaller and Weber too much for his finite mind to grasp.

In short, anarchy was loosed upon the brothers' world. They no longer knew any pleasure from eating, and now spent their hours at the table arguing over the best versions of a given dish, and how the one they had last week was better that the one in front of them. Every meal now bore the comparison of a thousand other competing versions, and their once-faithful happiness had been forever shattered by promiscuous researches all over town. Mr. Cutlets recounts their tale to spare some still-innocent palate the ravages of too much knowledge and the voracious maw of unrestrained appetite. If the fate of the seven brothers may be avoided at least once, the telling of their tale will have been worthwhile.

19 The Battle of Grilled Cheese and Bacon

Artisanal vs. Tony's Burger

Artisanal | 2 Park Ave. (at 32nd St.) | 212.725.8585
Tony's Burger | 34 E. 32nd St. | 212.779.7191

"The true gastronome," wrote Prosper Montagne, in his

monumental Larousse Gastronomique (1938), "while esteeming the most refined products of the culinary arts, enjoys them in moderation, and, for his normal fare, seeks out the simplest dishes, those which, moreover, are the most difficult to prepare to perfection." Every day testifies to the truth of this; take the grilled cheese and bacon sandwich. The Earl of Sandwich, whose unwillingness to leave his gaming table to eat is credited by a gullible posterity with causing the sandwich to be invented, never in his life dreamt of its power and beauty. A country like the United States, marked by nature with unheard-of bounty and unprecedented mobility, was bound to invent a lot of great sandwiches, and so we have: the hamburger, the submarine, the slider, the dagwood, and so on. It was an American who first put peanut butter and jelly together. It was an American who invented sliced bread! But the summit of American sandwich-making is undoubtedly the grilled cheese and bacon sandwich.

In its platonic form, the grilled cheese and bacon is probably the most perfect sandwich ever created. Three separate fats—margarine, milk fat, and savory bacon—conjoin to create a prism of greasy tastiness. Then there is the contrast between the smoky, salty sweetness of the bacon and the muted sharpness of the cheese. Finally, there is the exquisite opposition between the rugged crunch of bacon, and the viscous oneness of the cheese in which it is suspended—to say nothing of the contrast of both with carefully browned bread.

But how rarely is this American gem made correctly! Mr. Cutlets often finds himself in a queasy rage as he watches some insolent Bedouin desecrate a national treasure. First, the guy slaps undrained bacon onto waxy slices of cold cheese. Then he throws the half-assembled sandwich, without even a smear of margarine, onto the griddle. Leaving it to smolder for far too long, the cheese then turns into a liquid, bubbling horror, and when he slices it in half with the side of his filthy spatula, the hapless sandwich is nearly disemboweled. By this time, the only remaining value is in the crispness of the bread, and that is summarily ruined by wrapping it in a tight jacket of aluminum foil and wax paper, which serves to reduce it to a mushy paste.

For those who wish to avoid the above indignity of trying to destroy it at home, the classical version of the bacon and cheese sandwich can be had at practically any diner in the city; delis are less reliable. Generally, any place that serves a great bacon cheeseburger, such as Veselka or Big Nick's, can be counted upon to serve a fine version. (Exceptions persist though—both the Corner Bistro and McHale's overcook their bacon, the Corner Bistro actually deep-frying theirs.) One midtown take-out deli that does an exemplary job is the Chambord Royale, on 56th Street and Sixth Avenue, which also makes a fine hamburger. Unlike the burger, which will always be overcooked unless ordered rare, the grilled cheese is pitch-perfect, but be sure to open the plastic box before it overcooks. Avoid haute-bourgeois sandwiches, such as those at Ludlow Street's Grilled Cheese NY, like the plague; and if you can't get to a Greek diner, a fine panini is as close, in both spirit and matter, as you can get to the real thing, even if it doesn't quite fill the same hole in the soul.

Two versions of the grilled cheese and bacon sandwich, by two restaurants on opposite sides of 32nd Street, demonstrate for the whole world the maxim that there is beauty in simplicity. On the north side of the street is **Artisanal,** famed for its 250 varieties of cheese and its commitment to the best ingredients possible; and on the other side is **Tony's Burger,** a narrow and unassuming luncheonette. Both restaurants serve perfectly realized, conceptually opposed versions of the sandwich. And both versions have something to tell us.

Terrence Brennan's **Artisanal** is known for its elevated renditions of classic French comfort food, as well as its fanatical commitment to cheese. (At 250+, they are said to have the largest selection of cheese in America.) Artisanal's grilled cheese and bacon sandwich, made on Balthazar's pain au levain bread with English farmhouse cheddar and Nueske's applewood-smoked bacon, was anointed in 2002 by New York Magazine as the best in the city. It isn't bad, as the bread has a wonderfully resilient chomp to it, and the sharp English cheese, with its abundance of milk fat, goes well with the three-centimeter depth of butter. However, there are only trace elements of bacon in it, and, unfortunately, I generally don't bring a spectroscope to dinner.

But what's significant about Artisanal's sandwich, particularly taken alongside Tony's, is how comparatively crude it is. In every way, Tony's classical rendition—tangerine-colored square cheese on white bread, liberally margarined, with a core of four symmetrical strips of bacon—is more delicate, more artful, more balanced, and more restrained than its pompous rival. Take the bread. Artisanal's bread is coarse and thick, with gaping holes into which the melting cheese pools and burns. Tony's thin, Wonder-style bread, in contrast, is as light as air, and made of enriched bleached flour; it has practically refined itself out of existence, becoming a transparent vehicle for the taste and color of the golden-brown margarine crust. It's a gastronomic endpoint: compared with this, even the airiest baguettes are leaden loaves, and croissants peasant pumpernickel. Likewise, Tony's Indiana brand bacon is appropriately smoky; even if Artisanal had bothered to put some bacon in their pretentious sandwich, what would be the point of using apple-smoked Nueske's, an understated bacon sure to be overwhelmed by the pungent sharpness of the English cheese?

But hold on to your hat. I haven't even told you the worst part. I had to order the grilled cheese and bacon sandwich with a special instruction to "hold the apples." Apples! Yes, Artisanal, unless ordered otherwise, stuffs Granny Smith apple slices into its sandwich, attaining a level of grossness worthy of late-'70s Elvis. In fact, Mr. Cutlets would be hard-pressed to choose between the King's grilled peanut butter and banana creation and Artisanal's GC&B in a bad-taste contest.

Meanwhile, Tony stands behind his narrow counter, making perfect sandwiches, to little applause. But Mr. Cutlets sees—sees and appreciates.

Churrascaria Plataforma

316 W. 49th St. (bet. Eighth & Ninth Aves.) | 212.245.0505

💰💰💰

Meats of Note: all

The most common question Mr. Cutlets gets asked is unanswerable. "Mr. Cutlets," it begins, "what is the meatiest meal in all of New York?" Here I stall and equivocate. I point out the wondrous diversity of Manhattan's meats, and the subtle shadings of mood, appetite, and temperament that render the question meaningless. But this is so much show. There is a straight answer, which I have reserved only for my most serious acolytes. People want to believe that an ancient steak house, or venerable deli, is New York's most meat-intensive experience; and I can be forgiven for protecting them from the cruel truth. The ultimate New York meat meal is to be found at Churrascaria Plataforma, a Brazilian restaurant on a nondescript block with almost no trace of New York history and culture. Now you know. It's not what you would expect, but it is the truth.

Having awarded Churrascaria Plataforma the meaty laurels,

I will say that it isn't the best restaurant, nor the one I would choose for my last meal. But when it comes to sitting down and eating meat—not just feeding grossly on it, but enjoying its boundless grandeur, its exquisite diversity, its copiousness, its opulence, the play and interplay between meat and meat and cut and cut—there is nothing to compare to Churrascaria Plataforma.

The structure of a meal at Plataforma requires some explanation. It is a rodizio, or Brazilian barbecue, where the custom is for the waiters to bring freshly grilled pieces of meat around on skewers, slicing a little bit onto each plate. This "haven for meat lovers," as the restaurant describes itself, therefore has no real menu. It is simply a procession of cuts, one succeeding another like movements in some sublime symphony of meat. Prior to this Dionysian event, everyone takes their time picking through a vast appetizer buffet set up in the center of the restaurant. The pre-meat table, as I think of it, provides about as good a vegetarian meal as I can imagine: it includes everything from asparagus risotto to sashimi and marinated crab meat, along with half a dozen intriguing Brazilian specialty items. You could have a pretty good meal just helping yourself to lentils, octopus salad, quail eggs, and muqueca, the rich mahi-mahi and coconut milk stew beloved by South American grannies.

Once you have "primed the pump" and prepared your gastrointestinal system for the heroic exertions expected of it in the hours ahead, you order a caprininha, and turn your red coaster upside down. The green light tells the waiters to bring it on, and between the bright, limey sparkle of the potent cocktails and the sprightly music of the live bossa nova band, you are ready for the cavalcade of flesh to come. There's no particular order; the skewers come straight from the kitchen, and if you miss the savory pork tenderloin the first time round, you can be sure it will come out again. Generally, I like to start with the daintiest of skewered treats, such as the turkey wrapped in bacon, or the fabulous grilled spareribs. The beauty of the rodizio approach is that you can eat only the parts of the parts you like; you can direct the waiter to slice off just the blackened edge of a fibrous, fatty short rib, and then order a perfectly pink slice of flank steak to go with it.

Veal is succeeded by sausages, and sausages by sirloin, as the band plays on. The churrasco, or skirt steak, for which the restaurant is named, makes a cameo appearance, and even the "finny tribe" is represented, when a cart appears with a dense and elegant roasted salmon laid out upon it. The meat-man with a need to know can compare one kind of beef with another, arranging artful duos, trios, even quartets of cow, or, alternately, can create imaginative cross-carnal combos, either by taking a bite from each in succession, or even (especially after two or three caprihinas) creating tri-level meat sandwiches on your fork! Only in his most fervid ether dreams did Mr. Cutlets ever see himself taking such wild liberties with grilled meat, but that dream came true for me the day I sat down at Churrascaria Plataforma.

The parade goes on and on: chicken legs, lamb, then ham, and then . . . what's this? Could it be a whole towering skewer of crusty, medium-rare rib-eye steak? Yes! And one more caprihina, please. You might think you've about had it after finishing off your second or third menagerie of meats; but then that baby suckling pig rolls up on you, and there's nothing for it but to reach deep within and find the mettle to go on. Churrascaria Plataforma is an unconquerable challenge to even the hardiest of gluttons, but that doesn't mean you shouldn't at least give it your all. And when that extra gear does kick in, whether through alcohol, appetite, or sheer will, the committed carnophile can be fairly said to have consummated the ultimate act of meatliness.

Given all that, you would expect Churrascaria Plataforma to have attained some kind of legendary status among gluttons, or at the very least among cops, firemen, gym teachers, and other beefy types. But in fact, Churrascaria Plataforma barely registers on New York's food radar. Perhaps it is because of its assembly-line approach, so inimical to creative genius; or maybe because of the undeniably generic quality of the room, which for all its size and electricity, could as easily be in Cincinnati or Minsk as Manhattan. And it has to be said that, although almost every kind and cut of meat is served, they are all made in exactly the same way, which might bore some people not fixated on the study and appreciation of cooked animals. (Personally, I find it an invaluable control set for comparative analysis, but I'm kind of far-out that way.)

There are some serious shortcomings to Churrascaria Plataforma. I admit it. But at the end of the day, a restaurant is what they put in front of you. Churrascaria delivers meat, in limitless quantities and protean form, until you can hardly see. If that doesn't make it the ultimate New York meat meal, I don't know what does.

The years have not been kind to Mr. Cutlets. Once the haughtiest hostesses once clamored for my presence at galas, and veteran restaurateurs quailed at the thought of a hard word from my pen. My presence on Broadway was considered an omen of prosperity, and my robust carriage the ideal and measure of corpulent manhood. Today, however, Mr. Cutlets is a picture of penury, old and unloved, with only an unwholesome love of beef, pork, and veal keeping him from Potter's Field. And yet . . . as I stride on, moving manfully onward to my appointed hour, I look around me and see a city I helped to create. I see happy people, grasping sticks with seared and peppered flesh on the end, young women laughing over savory meat pies, and a hot dog in every child's tiny hand. Yes, though Mr. Cutlets wanes, New York waxes: a haven to any person with a dollar in his pocket and the love of meat in his heart. A cornucopia of ethnic snacks spill out onto the sidewalks and the streets.

KEBABS are New York's most visible street meat—to say nothing of their heavenly aroma, which often wafts half a block away, enticing office workers who had planned on salad. Generally, street kebabs are made up of economy cuts of beef, cut up and rubbed with pepper and other spices. You sometimes hear xenophobes grousing about the sinister likely origins of the meat, but you can do the math: it's a lot cheaper to buy chuck at C-Town than it is to go around trapping kitty cats. What gives kebabs their special zest is not the spices, though, or even the various sauces squirted on them as they cook. Make no mistake, the active element in kebabs is open flame. If you see them being cooked on a flat metal griddle, keep going. Eventually, you are bound to encounter the hot flames and encrusted grill that will give you the seared, sizzling flesh needed for the ultimate New York street accessory.

Ultimately you may end up at **Maria's Kebab Wagon** (14th Street and Sixth Avenue), whose charcoal grill, fresh sirloin tip beef, and bold spicing combine to make it the best in the city. Along with her son Gus, Maria Kosteanas has been a fixture on the corner for decades. "I've got customers that have been coming back for thirty years," she says. "I coat the meat with oregano, pepper, garlic pow-

der, and lemon sauce. The sauce has more spices in it, but that's a secret. I can't tell you about that. Then a little barbecue sauce or lemon juice as it cooks." The resulting meat ($2), appetizingly blackened and redolent of Maria's heady seasonings, can distract even the most purposeful pedestrians.

SOUVLAKI and SHWARMA, the kebab's more sophisticated cousins, are essentially Greek and Arab names for the same wonderful thing: a lamb or lamb/veal mixture that circulates in a tall, vertical rotisserie, and is served on pita bread with or without white yogurt sauce, tomatoes, lettuce, and onions. Just the outer edge of the meat is sliced, so essentially the sandwich is just the sizzling brown surface of a lamb roast! It seems too good to be true, but there it is. Now I hope that as you read this you are not thinking of the grayish-brown wads you've seen around town. That meat is a kind of rank, synthetic substance, pressed into a conical shape and served to the unsuspecting. The bona fide item looks like a lamb condominium, with hundreds of layers of sliced meat laid one upon another on the heavy spike. Their surfaces should be uneven, asymmetrical, and as beautiful as a stack of thousand-dollar poker chips. Try if at all possible to get shwarma at an off-hour (i.e., not when the bars close down). Nothing is more depressing than watching a crowd of drunks and ruffians gobble up all the brown surface, leaving you only the pale, bland meat beneath. Superb shwarma can be found at the **Yatagan Kebab House** at 104 MacDougal Street (between West 3rd and Bleecker Streets). **The Jerusalem Restaurant,** Broadway and 103rd Street, rivals it, although in a far less attractive neighborhood. **The Lite Touch on A,** 151 Avenue A (between Ninth and Tenth Avenues), is also very good.

CARRIBEAN-STYLE MEAT PIES are compact, clean, easy to eat, and pack a maximum load of meaty goodness in a small, cheap package. "You can eat them as you walk," says Kenneth Johnson, the manager of **Golden Krust** on 111 East 23rd Street. "Students like to eat them on the way to class." Golden Krust, at multiple locations around town, sells square pies, whose thick dough is crispy on the outside, and soft and dense as it comes closer to the velvety-smooth succulence of the beef filling, powered by Jamaican scotch bonnet peppers. The pies come in an open-ended little bag and fit perfectly in your hand. There is just enough meat to fill you up, but not enough to squeeze out when you bite it; paired with a cold grape soda, it's a world-class treat. Empanadas are Hispanic meat pies; they're milder, and usually filled with ground beef or chicken, often with some peas or olives slipped in to ameliorate the texture and taste. Their dough is flaky, rich, and supple, as there's not much filling to support. But empanadas, though less muscular than Jamaican meat pies, have a magic all their own. In no case, however, should you ever order one of the bright orange "meat pies" sold in pizzerias. You would do better to starve than to consume these insipid bug-baths.

HOT DOGS are universally regarded as a quintessential American food, but they're as German as lederhosen. That's why they flourish only in areas with large German-American or Ashkenazi Jewish populations, like Wisconsin or New York. People in places like Indiana and Uzbekistan, for example, don't know that a hot dog is supposed to be made of beef. They don't realize that it should have a natural casing that barely restrains a juicy meat charge, primed to explode at the first bursting bite. The sad souls in charge of most of the city's hot dog carts don't mean any harm by simmering a skinless dog in hot water all day until it resembles a decaying caterpillar. It's on you to do the right thing, and if at all possible, try to get a grilled natural-casing hot dog. There are dozens of **Nathan's** franchises around Manhattan, but they tend to be in depressing food courts, and their hot dogs invariably rest on stale, untoasted buns and cost nearly two dollars.

Almost as good, much cheaper, and a far more authentic New York hot dog experience can be had at **Gray's Papaya** and **Papaya King**. Gray's and Papaya King are almost identical operations, though both have fierce partisans. I for one find them pretty much equivalent, the Blur and Oasis of

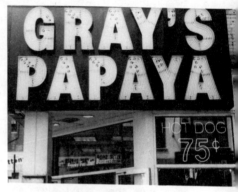

the hot dog world; essentially, both are hot dog stands that also sell a wide variety of tropical fruit drinks. I've never personally seen anyone order the tropical drinks, and I suspect they are there largely for show, like the toast and orange juice pictured in breakfast cereal advertisements, or the double-magnums of champagne displayed in cheap Italian restaurants. However, the ultra-sweet papaya drink does in fact go perfectly with a salty hot dog.

The essence of both places is the cheapness and exhilaration of the experience. If you can have a superb, snappy beef hot dog on a toasted bun with a cold drink for $2 or less (Gray's has been running a two-for-one "recession special" for years), then why shouldn't you have it again? A crew of glassy-eyed men slap dogs onto buns all day long, serving frankfurters with the efficiency of automatons. Many of the customers, particularly at the downtown Gray's, seem to be junkies; but really, what are we doing there except hitting the dummy pipe? If hot dogs are a drug, call me an addict! "One plain," I say, and the cashier responds, "One plain." The dog man says, "One plain," and I'm on the rock yet again. Papaya King closes at midnight, but you can "cop" at Gray's at any hour of the day or night.

But if Gray's and Papaya King are like crack, there is one place where you can get uncut 'caine: the wonderful **Hallo Berlin** (54th Street and Fifth Avenue) wurst cart. Billing itself as "the wurst pushcart in New York," this admirable oasis, run by Rolf Babiel, takes the hot dog back to its source: bratwurst, knockwurst, alpenwurst, and other superb Shaller and Weber sausages, sold either on a bun or sliced up with winy red cabbage. The sauerkraut is fantastic, as are other German treats like red cabbage and German fried potatoes. Babiel's "German soul food" is so popular that it has actually spawned two sit-down restaurants, but he maintains the cart even so. This would be a better city with a Hallo Berlin on every corner. Someday, as Travis Bickle said, a real rain will come and wash all the scum away.

There are other food carts in New York City that definitely deserve a stop by if you're in the neighborhood. (Or a little journey if you're not.)

Jane's Cart > Central Park South

Walking in Central Park with one of Jane's immense sandwiches and a cold Yoo-Hoo is probably as much happiness as this world allows. That doesn't mean that it's cheap, though. Both the rib-eye steak sandwich and the equally succulent pork loin come in at a whopping eight dollars. Loaded with sautéed peppers and mushrooms, and served on a thick and tender grilled pita, they're more than enough for two. (Ask for two forks.) The chicken is almost as good, as are the sausage sandwiches; but steer clear of the overpriced burgers, which skyrocket in price if you add bacon. Jane's freshly made muffins and other baked goods are also superb.

Rahman's Kwik Meal > 45th St. & Sixth Ave.

Muhammed Rahman was formerly a chef at the Russian Tea Room, and he brings a level of technical mastery to his lamb and chicken dishes that you don't usually see in a street cart. But all the credit, he says, goes to his mom in Bangladesh. "She was a great cook," he says. "She would marinate the lamb with raw unripe papaya, and I do too." The lamb also takes a bouquet of spices, including onion, garlic, ginger, cumin, and coriander. Served either with basmati rice or on a pita, and dressed with jalapeño peppers and yogurt sauce, it's attracted a wildly loyal following all around town. "People make special trips to eat my lamb, shrimp, and chicken," Rahman says. One customer was even inspired to write the Kwik Meal a poem, which is posted on the stand's rear wall: "Cooked to perfection by expert hands / Striving to meet the customers' demands." Mr. Cutlets couldn't say it better himself.

The Squid Lady > Hester and Bowery

This busy stand, on a busy corner on Chinatown's northern frontier, definitely presents non-Chinese people with a challenge. All the food is hidden by lids, the descriptions are all in Chinese, and the harried woman who runs the cart barely speaks a word of English. One word she does know, however, is "squid." Her pungent, al dente curried squid, served along with a dollop of sauce over thick, ropy noodles ($2), is one of the city's great hidden treats. Just make sure you get plenty of napkins, and then find a place where you can get busy eating it. Curried squid is not the neatest food in the world to eat while you're walking.

Numerous **DELI BUFFETS** all over town offer mobile meats, many of which are completely disgusting. Once in a while, though, you can stumble across something great. When that happens, there is nothing to do but ladle several servings into a little plastic box, grab a Yoo-Hoo, and head for the nearest curb. But rather than pontificate further, Mr. Cutlets though it might be easier to just offer some helpful rules of thumb when approaching the world of the deli buffet:

- The meats that flourish best at deli buffets are the fatty ones that can withstand the hours of exposure to warm air. In some cases, as with the gloppy-sweet and sticky ribs, don't bother. But with others, the long steam-tray sit serves it well—better, in fact, than the kitchen might have hoped for. Long hours of low heat ossify the outsides of these meats, reducing their surfaces to parched deserts, which neatly contain the moist richness still hidden beneath. The lukewarm temperature also contrives with their protective dry sheathing to make deli buffet meats the ultimate finger food!

- Among the best buffet meats to look for are meat loaf in gravy, Cuban roast pork, roast chicken, Swedish meatballs, sausages, any kind of Salisbury steak, and fried chicken thighs. Give the other parts of the fried chicken a wide berth; they taste dried out and leathery, and the breading is stale. Likewise, keep clear of any other fried foods, which have the briefest of blooms.

- As with all street food, make sure you get plenty of napkins. These delis are in the habit of doling them out one by one, like lottery tickets, and they are far too skimpy to be of any use except in bunches. Another problem lies in the plastic containers they use. If, like Mr. Cutlets, you like to take a minute sample of five or six different meats, each with its own tiny dollop of sauce, nothing could be more foul than seeing them all slimed up together, turning a mini-banquet into a chum slick. An ingenious solution is to take a small container, spread it open, and then fill in both sides with separate dishes. Then take another small container, reverse it, and fasten the first one closed: you now have a side-by-side portion-controlled street meat holder, courtesy of the mind of Mr. Cutlets! Repeat as necessary.

Remember, a creative and industrious gourmand is the greatest enemy bad food can know. If you set your mind to it, a good meal is possible everywhere, with any resources. Even at the humblest delis, the possibilities are beguiling: meat loaf and gravy on a toasted bialy; turkey skin, roast chicken, and fresh peas on a pumpernickel bagel; sausage and macaroni and cheese on a kaiser roll. Just don't give up, and always keep the counsel of Mr. Cutlets in your ear!

Les Halles

411 Park Ave. South (bet. 28th & 29th Sts.) | 212.679.4111

💰💰💰💰

Meats of Note: hangar steak, prime rib, pig feet

HANGAR STEAK

Les Halles has been called a French steak house, but that's misleading: there could never be such a thing as a French steak house. Despite the fact that they literally invented the idea of eating steak and fried potatoes for dinner, our friends across the pond would never make a virtue of mere quantity and crudeness. When I was a young man, my father took me to "ring the gong" at a Parisian meatery called Moulin a Vent. The place was a legitimate restaurant, but its dedication to meat was beyond question. Its limousin contrefilet was unforgettable, festooned as it was with an unforgotten Bordelaise. To this day, the shallots, wine, and beefy blood merge in my mind with the oil paintings of raw beef that covered the walls.

Neither the sauce nor the still lifes would ever show up in an American steak house, but that's only the beginning of the difference. The French butcher their meat differently, cook it differently, and relate to it differently than do Americans. It's neither a totem of manhood nor a fetish item for depressed dieters, as in the USA. Chef Anthony Bourdain, since becoming a food-media star, has taken a fairly wide license with his newfound fame, and has alienated many of his peers with his high-handed and unabashedly mercantile ways. But whatever else one thinks of him, the guy has managed to incarnate (so to speak) French meat sensibilities into a New York restaurant. Les Halles' commitment to French meat ways earns it a high place in Mr. Cutlets' clogged heart. How can you not love a Park Avenue restaurant with a brightly lit meat counter right next to the host podium?

"Do you know the back story with French butchers?" Bourdain once asked me. We were talking about hangar steak, one of his favorite media. "The French have gone for it for years, because cutting meat in France is very different. There's only one slaughterhouse, and maybe there's one steer in town. So they have to make do, and become resourceful and enterprising in using every cut. Hangar steak is one of those cases where you sacrifice a little tenderness for flavor. It's so much more interesting than filet mignon. It has a ropy texture, and a stronger, slightly kidneyish flavor that I love." Bourdain seems to be in a scholarly reverie, like a rabbi explaining a particularly knotty problem in Maimonides. But then he quickly snaps out of it, reverting back to a hard-boiled observer of the restaurant scene. "Of course, it's clearly a hot menu item right now."

Bourdain's entrepreneurial instincts don't get in the way of his restaurant's approach to meat. The hangar steaks, like most of his other meats, are grilled expertly and served with classical accompaniments: in this case, a hot, winy Béarnaise that brought back memories of Moulin a Vent. The filet steak, as bland and pointless in France as it is here, is enlivened somewhat by an orthodox Béarnaise. The faux-fillet, cousin to the New York Strip, is such a robust piece of beef that New York steak houses, from Sparks on down, almost invariably serve it stark naked, but Les Halles tops it with Bordelaise butter; the result is spectacular, although you have to wonder why the classic sauce wouldn't do just as well. A sop to the marketplace, perhaps? The steak frites, on the other hand, sacrifices nothing to local prejudice. It's nothing more or less than a rump steak, an old-time economy cut almost never seen in New York anymore.

On the other end of the economic scale, Les Halles serves a magnificent Cote du Boeuf (prime rib) for two. This is probably one of the most gratifying meals you can eat, and a triumph of intercontinental meat engineering. It is a majestic presentation, vastly more appetizing than the usual soggy slab of roast beef Americans are accustomed to seeing arrive in a bath of juice. The twisted, irregular french fries, all salt and crunchy starch, are another Gallic masterstroke. But on the other hand, no cow that ever grazed on French grass can compete with the best American Black Angus cattle, and this Cote du Boeuf is certified Angus down to its marrow. ("It's all about the fat," Bourdain told me of the exquisitely marbled Angus meat. "That's where the taste is.") It really is something special. I love Les Halles' breaded, brown pigs feet, the juicy free-range chicken for two, and the rugged hangar steak, with its nostalgic (to me) wine-and-shallot sauce; but when that prime rib comes out, oh boy!

Forget about the franchise, and ignore Bourdain's books. Les Halles is one of New York's great meat restaurants. France never had a better ambassador in the history of the corps diplomatique.

23 Oh, You Kid!

A guide to goat

Goat is the least popular of barnyard animals, despite having a tender meat that doesn't taste very different from lamb. But then, lamb has a cultural heritage going back to antiquity, whereas we associate goat with rank and unhygienic societies. But goat's special flavor stands up especially well to the spicier cuisines of the world, which is one reason it figures so prominently in the Mexican, Indian, and Carribbean canons.

A roasted kid, either spit- or oven-, is a great treat, but rarely seen: even at l'Impero, which boasts of "roasted capretto," the meat is closer to a stew than a roast, with no browned fat to be found. More often, goat is served in curries, stews, and other long-simmering dishes. **Dawat's** (210 E. 58th Street, 212.355.7555) home-style goat, for example, is simmered with cardamom sauce, as is **Bombay Harbour**'s (72-32 Broadway, Queens, 718.898.5500) Dhaka Hazi's biryani, which features tender morsels of kid in a pile of spiced rice redolent of mustard oil. (Goat is largely an outer borough treat, which is one reason it is underrepresented in this book.) The most goat-centric restaurant I know of is Coney Island's **Los Mariachis** (805 Coney Island Boulevard, Brooklyn, 718.826.3388), a good-time Mexican place that happens to serve barbecued goat, goat stew, oven-baked goat, and even goat broth.

Given today's rococo preparations and crazy-man-crazy seasonings, you would think goat's time had come. It has a world-food cache, too. More people in the world eat goat than beef; though unfortunately almost none of them dine out. Which is a shame. Because goat, like mutton, has a stronger, more assertive, and more complex taste all around than lamb, meatier and more muscular, which, sadly, hasn't even begun to be explored by New York's chefs—at least in Manhattan.

Daniel / Café Boulud

Daniel | 60 E. 65th St. | 212.288.0033

$ $ $ $

Café Boulud | 20 E. 76th St. (bet. Fifth & Madison) | 212.772.2600

$ $ $ $

DANIEL BOULUD

Daniel Boulud, whose genius and ambition have made Daniel one of the world's great restaurants, loves to talk about meat. From the tete de veau (cow's head) he has made for friends, to the eight-course pot-au-feu meal he occasionally works up (with each ingredient getting a full-dress treatment from the kitchen), Boulud is New York's preeminent meat-man. His gastronomic vocabulary is vast, his stature titanic, and his creativity proverbial, but Boulud's feeling for flesh is as elemental as any steak mogul's. Though Vongerichten may have a more prodigious vocabulary of flavor, or Ripert a more delicate sensibility, Boulud is the most grounded, the most organic, and the most profound chef in New York City for Mr. Cutlets' money. He is the meat-master, with no equal in the arts of preparing animal tissue for human consumption. He is my man.

Of what does Boulud's genius consist? Dinner at Daniel answers all questions as to his particular brilliance. Boulud's signature style, if it can be called that, involves simultaneous deployment of the most flamboyant and rarefied culinary artistry with a completely grounded, organic sensibility. His ventures are invariably accompanied by much fanfare about his farm-boy childhood, or of his parents' rustic restaurant in Lyons. But in Boulud's case, these bona fides are more than just marketing hype. "There's always something you can do," he told me once, when I asked him about the immense staff meals. "The most important thing as a chef is not to throw anything out." He'll tell you how his favorite vegetable is a potato, or about all the "little cuts" French butchers developed because, in France, there was generally one butcher for a village, and you had to stretch a carcass. Or how his grandmother's chicken fricassee was better with tough old hens, the kind you can't serve in restaurants. In may ways, Boulud is a bubba, a good old boy, and his wildest flights of imagination as a chef all take off from a clearing in the forest. As a result, you never know what he will come up with: Over the course of one meal, Boulud may produce a marvel like his sea scallop ceviche in an oyster-water nage touched with horseradish, lime and sea urchin, all shiny sea and dappled sunshine, and follow it with his rabbit and foie gras "Galantine" with morels, pickled spring onion, wild aspargus with "Colza" dressing, and a chervil rabbit gelée, a huntsman's idyll. The New York Times' William Grimes, upon giving Daniel his long-awaited four-star review, expressed this nicely: "Mr. Boulud's style," wrote Grimes, "is a seductive blend of qualities, robust and delicate at the same time, like a big-engine car that hits top speed with the merest toe-touch on the accelerator." But to the power of his skill, Grimes also singled out for praise Boulud's daring in working "wrong side of the track" ingredients into haute dishes, citing his mind-boggling braised pork belly and stuffed pig's trotters served with lentils and root vegetables in a black truffle jus.

"For me, meat has a great role to play," Boulud says. "Great chefs have to have that balance. The meat isn't just a blank slate; it has to come through. That's one reason I like pork, which absorbs spices without being covered up. At Daniel, we frequently prepare 'duos' or 'trios' or 'epigrams' of different meats. With lamb, this may mean a slice of roasted saddle stuffed with Swiss chard and tomato confit, a piece of braised shoulder, and a chop from a roasted rack. One of my signature dishes is a duo of beef and celery that pairs roasted tenderloin with boneless short ribs braised in red wine [and braised celery stalks with a celery root-potato purée]. I like creating preparations like this because they let the guest savor lamb, for example, in different ways with different tastes and textures."

If Daniel is Boulud's Carnegie Hall, then Café Boulud, his second restaurant, is his downtown performance space, an experimental staging area for dishes made in his baroque-pastoral mode. Andrew Carmellini, the unassuming young American whom Boulud chose to run Café Boulud, has a similar sensibility. "I think it's really worked out because we feel the same way about things. We both like to cook passionately, but in a rooted kind of way. We never really did musical cooking . . . it's gotta have soul." Unlike Daniel's exquisitely conceived dishes, though, which seem so natural and inevitable that it's hard to believe they were invented at all, Café Boulud's offerings are brilliant but erratic, thrown off constantly in the heat of inventiveness. "Every night I run six or seven specials," Carmellini told me, not without a trace of pride. "Every night." Some, like a country style pâté with foie gras and smoked duck, dried fig chutney, and a purslane-frisée salad, are spectacular; others may underwhelm. But the privilege of being exposed to such constant experimentation can't help but excite.

One reason why Café Boulud requires so many new dishes is its menu, which is divided into four sections. "La Tradition," which is probably the strongest, includes such tried-and-true classics as Boulud's chicken Grand-mere Francine, and the aforementioned fricassee, whose succulent Amish chicken, exquisitely powerful broth, and exquisitely paired bacon and mushroom backgrounders have given so many diners nostalgia for a boyhood they never had. "Le Voyage" gives Carmellini his widest scope, allowing him ingredients and techniques from all over the world; he really lets himself go with this one. "La Saison" stresses seasonal delicacies and is the home of some of the restaurant's most perfect creations (that day's was an herb-crusted John Dory that almost made me go over to seafood). Even the weakest of the four, "Le Potager" (vegetarian) had both noble failures and home runs on it.

What Daniel, Café Boulud, and Boulud's third restaurant, the sleek, underrated DB Bistro Moderne, have in common, however, is their singular ability to please both the most elevated, as well as the most elemental, tastes. Whereas some chefs have carved out specific demesnes for themselves, or this or that sector of the restaurant-going public, Boulud, along with his lieutenants, has taken the whole measure of human appetites and given it back for all the world to enjoy. When it comes to odd spices and unexpected flavorings, even a Vongerichten loyalist will grant that Boulud is a master. All his restaurants have vast and judicious cellars, impeccable cheese carts, and hair-raisingly good desserts. (Francois Payard was his original patissier.) Even if these names don't mean anything to you, the message should get through. Boulud is, if not the best of all chefs, certainly the easiest to love, and the one who seems to love meat the most. If Mr. Cutlets could be any chef, it would be Boulud; and if I ever found the perfect meat, it would be he whom I would want cooking it. I doubt I will ever find the perfect meat; but there can be no higher compliment, as I strive onward in my search.

26 Seats

168 Avenue B (bet. 10th & 11th Sts.) | 212.677.4787

$ $ $

Meats of Note: duck, venison, chicken

26 Seats is the kind of restaurant whose loss pains New York's exiles most. There's no taking anything away from the city's most celebrated restaurants, the Daniels or Nobus; but people in New York don't really eat in those places any more frequently than do out-of-towners. No, what makes New York the hemisphere's restaurant mecca is the existence of places like 26 Seats—tiny local restaurants good and dependable enough to dine at two or three times a week. In any other city, 26 Seats would be one of the "top spots for romance" announced on the cover of a glossy city magazine; here, it's just a place in the neighborhood.

Of course, it's a place that is filled with good eaters, day and night, including a regular quota of French nationals—always a good sign. And it's not like 26 Seats is on the beaten path: owner Corinne Deysson and her husband, Bernard, run this mom-and-pop operation on an out-of-the-way block in Alphabet City. The restaurant differs from most of the insouciant bistros dotting Avenue B, though, in representing, along with funky decorating style, complete mastery of basic French food. Simply stated, Bernard can flat-out cook. This isn't obvious from reading the menu, which superficially resembles many other, lesser joints. But as always, you can tell in the way they handle meats just how sure-handed and inventive 26 Seats is.

The chicken is a good example. Restaurants have to put chicken on the menu, but for many, their hearts just aren't in it. Rarely do you see a chicken dish as thoughtful (or as good) as the house's best beef or pork dishes. 26 Seats, though, serves a crisp-skinned chicken breast, cut into thick, succulent slices and lightly dressed with an assertive, but not overwhelming, mustard-Sauterne sauce. The duck breast is, like everything else here, simple and superb, both in terms of the quality of the meat (as robust and electric as aged beef) and the preparation (pan-seared, then fanned out rare with a simple cherry-inflected pan jus). On the winter menu, the restaurant serves a wide variety of specials, including a rich lamb shank over white beans, perfectly cooked and plated quail, and a marinated venison tenderloin to beat all comers. The venison is the best of the lot: marinated in wine, it's pan-seared, black-peppered, and served with a subdued port sauce. It's just gamy enough to stand up to the sauce, and so meltingly tender that it's hard to think of it as game.

26 Seats also serves admirable renditions of seared trout, steak au poivre, and other understated and fulfilling classics. All the desserts are better than they have to be, particularly a robust dark chocolate mousse and a delicate apple tart. The whole feel of the place—the familiarity of the owners, the mismatched chairs and multicolored walls, the eclectic mix of music overhead—makes it an ideal neighborhood haunt for a person who wants every meal, even local ones, to be an event.

ápizz

217 Eldridge St. (bet. Rivington & Stanton Sts.) | 212.253.9199

💰 💰 💰

Meats of Note: meatballs, lasagna with wild boar ragu

ápizz is a small restaurant on an as-yet-ungentrified street on the Lower East Side. It has no windows, and a door suitable to keeping out King Kong guards the entrance. Inside, the place has the fugitive warmth and comfort of a refugee camp—but an elegant one. It's wholly representative of its era—low "comfort foods" are served here with an almost baroque refinement and artifice. (A sister restaurant is called "Peasant," and takes a similar Marie-Antoinette-and-her-milkmaids approach.)

ápizz is meant to take southern Italian cookery as its theme, with an emphasis on wood-oven baking. The oven is in fact a wonderful instrument. Stoked with cherry wood, it imparts a smoky, pleasantly fruity taste to everything that goes in it, even for a few minutes, like the crisp pizza and the firm, fresh calamari. But the meats that matter at ápizz have only a tangential relation to the oven. First and foremost are the meatballs, which have quickly built a reputation as the best around—outclassing even John's, the venerable red sauce joint on 12th Street, which was widely known for this spherical specialty. For Mr. Cutlets' money, there is a fairly fixed ceiling on how good a meatball can be, and many restaurants in Manhattan attain it—to say nothing of even better places in Brooklyn and the Bronx. But there is no denying ápizz a place in the city's meatball aristocracy. The meatballs at ápizz are so good that they don't even bother serving them with spaghetti. They just show up, each about the size of an orange, in red sauce, partially stuffed with fresh ricotta. Their veal-pork-beef mixture is too dense, and their sheer size too large, for the smoke to make much headway into the meat, but that's all right. They are absolutely perfect on their own, unmarred by any unwarranted spicing, and served in an equally simple, and equally superb, ultra-fresh tomato sauce. The fresh ricotta doesn't add much to the taste, but its creaminess helps relieve the granular monotony of so much . . . meatball.

Also not to be missed at ápizz, particularly for pork-gatherers, is the lasagna with wild boar ragu. I don't know if this is authentic, or innovative, or what, but it's unlike any other lasagna I've had, owing both to its construction (the only cheese present is crumbled parmesan) and the gamy, rich ragu. Boar is an interesting taste—like pork, but funkier, more aggressive—and thus better able to stand up to the off-setting tastes of sweet tomato and salty parmesan, the other two primary ingredients in this pyramid-powered winner. Boar is basically pork squared, much as mutton is to lamb; so if you don't like the taste of pork, stay away and order one of the pastas. ápizz's pork chops and chicken, though they look great, tend to be overcooked and dried out. The lamb chops were not, but didn't recommend themselves otherwise.

Artie's Deli

2290 Broadway (at 83rd St.) | 212.579.5959

Meats of Note: flanken in a pot, chicken soup,
stuffed cabbage, salami burger

Artie's Deli was the brainchild of Artie Cutler, the same
visionary restaurateur who gave the world Ollie's, Gabriela's,
Carmine's, Virgil's, and a number of other superb ethnic-

niche restaurants, all enormous, reliable, smoothly run, and
absolutely true to their sources. Artie's was the very last, as
Cutler died before the place could be opened. But it's completely in keeping with his other restaurants. So much so, in
fact, that you need some experience with Jewish cooking to
really enjoy it. People who visit Artie's in search of an ultimate Pastrami experience are bound to come away disappointed, because Artie's pastrami and corned beef are just
adequate, like most tourist-driven deli restaurants. But
Artie's real value lies in its blue-ribbon renditions of such
yiddishe standards as flanken in a pot, chicken soup, and
stuffed cabbage.

Of the flanken, I have already spoken (see chapter 13, The

Beef Less Eaten). The chicken soup is almost exactly what you would get if you had the good fortune to be sick and under the care of a Jewish grandmother. Other delis, like the Carnegie, have refined their chicken soup into a heavenly consommé, as clear and unpolluted as optical glass. Artie's gives you the hamishe (homey) version, with carrots, celery, tiny sprigs of dill, various other herb particles, and even the precious "gold coins" (circlets of fat) that have opened the alveoli of so many sick children. There is also a diaphanous, softball-size matzoh ball, but it is inessential. This is great soup, and the better for not being so refined. Likewise, the stuffed cabbage is vast, grainy, greasy, rich, and utterly, utterly delicious. So much ground beef and Minute Rice is stuffed inside immense cabbage leaves that you wonder how they did it; the raisin-studded tomato gravy, however, presents no mysteries. Artie's is one of the best restaurants to eat in for sick people: it presents no problems or contradictions, and there's usually a sensitive soul at a nearby table that will inquire after your well-being. It's also completely representative of modern Jewish restaurants in that almost no one who works there seems to be Jewish.

One of the restaurant's most far-out dishes, which deserves special discussion, is the underappreciated salami burger, which should be a great latter-day contribution to deli food. Mr. Cutlets, in his boyhood, used to console himself on many a loveless night with the wonderful Maynard Burger served at Maynard's bar, in Margate, N.J. The Maynard Burger was a cheeseburger topped with a thick slice of grilled pork roll. It was like a bacon cheeseburger, but richer, softer, more voluptuous, and more satisfying. And what is pork roll (or Taylor ham, as it is sometimes called) but a poor man's beef salami? The spontaneous reinvention of the Maynard Burger in a Manhattan deli was enough to send Mr. Cutlets into a rapture of human brotherhood—until my salami burger came out, that is, with cold, waxy salami slices piled crudely on top. Artie's couldn't come all the way—but you can, if you ask, or rather insist, that the salami be grilled before crowning the burger. In a way, the salami burger needs to come to fruition. The history of Jewish cooking is grounded in carefully cooked, fatty meats, after all, and its future will be, too.

Artisanal

2 Park Ave. (at 32nd St.) | 212.725.8585

Meats of Note: cassoulet toulousain

Artisanal would seem to be an unlikely candidate for Mr. Cutlets' attentions. Terrence Brennan's popular restaurant is famous primarily for its cheeses. There are over 250, of every

imaginable type, and many of the dishes on the menu revolve around them. But Artisanal also features a number of classic bistro dishes on its menu, and it occurred to me that a restaurant so whole-heartedly committed to cheese would have its heart in the right place when it came to meat.

And this assumption was more or less borne out. Only in the matter of steak did Artisanal let me down. Their prime hangar steak consists of a child's portion of meat—an unforgivable lapse with this economy cut. It comes out covered with french fries, as if the kitchen were ashamed to be charging $22 for it. A beaufort cheese and bacon tart had hardly enough bacon to wrap a scallop in, but the mild cheese and delicate phyllo-like crust was far closer in both form and spirit to an ideal grilled cheese and bacon sandwich than the restaurant's actual version of that dish, which I abhor. (See chapter 19, The Battle of Grilled Cheese and Bacon.) A large and tender, if not especially vivid, Jamison Farms lamb shank was elevated by its accompaniment, a goat cheese polenta.

The kitchen was shown to best effect by its specials. Cassoulet toulousain, the traditional white-bean casserole, is practically a rhapsody of meat: the white beans are essentially just vehicles for meat juices, which in this version include bacon, garlic sausage, duck confit, and smoked pork shoulder. All of these melt into the beans, which are then topped with a cheese-infused breadcrumb crust. At other times, Artisanal has featured pig's trotters, a very respectable rabbit au Riesling, and an exemplary rendition of coq au vin. For definitive renditions of classic bistro dishes, I still prefer Balthazar; but for a cheese restaurant, Artisanal still has its heart in the right place—or at least its cassoulet.

Balthazar

80 Spring St. (bet. Crosby and Broadway) | 212.965.1785

💰 💰 💰

Meats of Note: short ribs, roast chicken for two,
prime rib for two

Balthazar enjoyed a long vogue in the mid-to-late 1990s as the gathering place of the glitterati, the place where Puffy, J. Lo, Jesse Camp, and other Clinton-era "stars" came to see and be seen. Afterward, the restaurant settled into a blue-giant period, with occasional celebrity sightings, plentiful tourist traffic, and a devoted clientele of serious eaters who appreciated its faithful homage to classic French brasserie cooking. Owner Keith McNally has spared no expense in try-ing to re-create, in loving and minute detail, the Parisian late-night restaurants like Paris's Brasserie Balzar that are its inspiration. High ceilings, immense wall-mounted wood mirrors, and sleek banquettes mark the big room; in the air there is a bright electricity of noise and bustle. Everyone seems happy, drinking carafes of the house Beaujolais and talking happily over steak frites. The staff is faultlessly brisk, attentive, and invisible, except when they are carrying five-foot tiered pyramids of shellfish. (Then they look like aquari-ums with legs.)

Balthazar's menu is big, and without a single bad dish as far as I can tell. Meat-eaters in particular will glory in its choic-es. The steak frites are a classic rendition; and such imagi-native, homey dishes as duck shepherd's pie, cassoulet, and lamb shanks have a casual, no-pressure presentation that belies the effort and intelligence that went into making these compound dishes exactly right. Frissee aux lardoons (chico-ry salad with bacon and eggs) is fabulously light and fluffy, with bright, light lettuce perfectly suited to dressing with poached egg, and thick cubes of smoky but soft bacon. A grilled pork chop with a prune-armanac sauce is uncured, unbrined, and delicious, if a little overcooked. Duck confit is a hymn to crisp poultry fat, dry on the outside, succulent beyond belief on the inside. It's salty and fatty, and comes with fried potatoes and lush wild mushrooms. The Saturday night special, braised short ribs, is even more elementally gratifying. With its rich, soft, fibrous meat and potent, winey sauce, it requires absolutely zero effort to appreciate. You can be almost completely in the bag from drinking Beaujolais, and the short ribs will still find a direct line to your brain stem. They're that good.

Probably the most spectacular dishes at Balthazar, though, are the big dinners for two—roast chicken and prime rib. The chicken is a thing of perfect simplicity: there's no black truffles stuffed up its sleeve, or any other culinary flourishes. It's just a delicious free-range chicken, of vivid flavor and freshness, roasted just right, and rolled out on a cart in all its golden glory, before being returned to the kitchen to be cut up. The cotes de boeuf are naturally a much more formidable presentation, and one that any beefeater will find frankly pornographic in its visual appeal. Could it look any bigger, browner, more robustly rare on the inside, with a long, jagged bone arcing along its length? Holy cow! Like the chicken, the cote du boeuf is brought back and cut up for you, but there is no moment quite like its arrival. To a dedicated meat-eater, it's a more riveting sight than Puff Daddy any day.

Carmine's

200 W. 44th St. | 212.221.3800
2450 Broadway | 212.362.2200

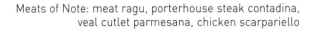

Meats of Note: meat ragu, porterhouse steak contadina,
veal cutlet parmesana, chicken scarpariello

There aren't many men whom Mr. Cutlets can call "hero." Gennaro Lombardi, the father of pizza in America. Jonas Salk. The "sausage and egg hermit," a celebrated recluse whose monastic devotion to the same meal three times a day for fifteen years eventually led to thrombotic martyrdom. And to this list I must add the late Artie Cutler (no relation). A visionary with boundless powers of execution, Cutler created, in the course of a few short years, five completely faithful homages to five different cuisines, and was in the midst of creating a sixth, Artie's Deli, when he was called to his reward in 1998. Each restaurant is immense, affordable, and beautiful, with faultless service and a vast and authentic menu.

Carmine's is Cutler's interpretation of the old-time red-sauce joint. I like it better than the places it emulates. That's a vaguely shameful thing to admit. No doubt there are old-timey restaurants in Little Italy, the Bronx, or Nova Zembla that are better than Carmine's. They should be better. But like Lays of Ancient Rome or Miller's Crossing, the parody is all too often better than the original—wider-ranging, more knowing, and generous to the point of extravagance with the qualities you like best.

Take Carmine's ragu. It's not too hard to see that the foundation of any red-sauce restaurant is the red sauce. Carmine's is delicious, although not particularly outstanding. But their meat gravy is positively monumental. Four kinds of meat cavort in a joyous dance together: big, delicately spiced, pork-and-veal inflected meatballs; stout, porky sausages from Faicco's pork store; exquisite, classically-constructed braciole; and, wonder of wonders, melting pieces of fibrous, rich flanken, the king of tender, fatty meats. This is red-sauce restaurant ragu, a far cry from the austere, velvety-smooth substance perfected by the Bolognese over the centuries; no contrast between northern and southern Italian food could be more telling. Mr. Cutlets always counted himself in the northern camp, until Carmine's showed me the folly of my way.

Carmine's other meat dishes, while less revelatory, are equally sumptuous. An immense porterhouse steak of the very highest quality is served festooned with Faicco sausage and potatoes and drizzled with vinegar juice. Veal parmesan is an immense, perfectly sautéed swath of delicate, juicy cutlet, thick and yet fork-tender; it goes down as easily as pudding, and despite its immense size (like everything at Carmine's, it's intended to be shared by three people) can all too easily be eaten in a sustained burst of enthusiasm. Nearly everything on the menu at Carmine's is exceptional, but one other dish deserves special mention: the Chicken Scarpariello, described on Carmine's website as "served on the bone, marinated and sautéed until crispy with a sauce of roasted garlic, rosemary, oregano, white wine, butter, chicken stock, and lemon." This haiku hardly does justice to the dish itself, but then the same could be said for my own poor powers. If only the late Mr. Cutler had a worthy eulogist! Until then, I can only keep eating at Carmine's (and Virgil's, and Ollie's) in his memory.

City Hall

131 Duane St. (bet. W. Broadway and Church St.) | 212.227.7777

💰 💰 💰

Meats of Note: blade steak, skirt steak, rib for two

In any other city, a restaurant as strikingly beautiful as City Hall would be more well known. Set on a TriBeCa side street, and art-directed in the most opulent way by the owner of SoHo's gorgeous Cub Room, City Hall specializes in the preparation of great beef. In some cases, as with the sublime skirt steak, the flavorful meat is matched with a simple dressing including some unexpected capirs; in other cases, as with the unfortunate del-monico, a hunk of revolting Maytag Blue Cheese imposes itself so forcefully that you can hardly taste the meat—a fact that isn't helped by the relative blandness of the steak. The hamburger couldn't be any better, and the rib steak for two is a spectacle worthy of a special detour. And of course the towering, multi-tiered platters of shellfish make me proud to live here.

But the real reason I include City Hall in this guide is their inclusion of a rare-as-plutonium top blade steak on its menu. Mr. Cutlets has always been enamored of economy cuts.

The top blade steak is cheap even by their standards. Also called a book steak or butler steak, and here called a flatiron steak, it's cut from an especially large and lean part of the always under-rated chuck (shoulder and neck) section. The top blade steak is a cut from a top blade roast, a tasty if tough cut high up on the shoulder. Despite this toughness, it is surprisingly edible, particularly when cut across the grain. City Hall serves a flatiron steak with a wet little chimichurri, but it really isn't necessary at all. The steak, without an iota of external fat, and no more marbling than a tomato, is simultaneously lean and juicy, with a tender resiliency reminiscent of cross-cut flank steak. As a rule of thumb, no restaurant that serves something that humble can ever be accused of indifference to the meaty arts. On that account alone—along with its sweeping staircases, burnished wood, beautiful bar and large outdoor tables—you can't fight City Hall.

Delta Grill

700 Ninth Ave. (at 48th St.) | 212.956.0934

                     $ $

Meats of Note: chicken-fried steak

One summer some years go, after an especially orgiastic feeding at Churrascaria Plataforma, I stumbled out onto 49th Street, blinking in the moist darkness of the August night. I walked up the block in the hope that the lights and sounds of Ninth Avenue might wake me from the sated haze that had come over me. My constitutional had not taken me more than a single block when I noticed a promising-looking southern restaurant with a number of appealing specials on a chalkboard outside. Barely able to feel my extremities by now, I hailed a passing ambulance, but with my last conscious act made a mental note to try the place after I had recovered from the debauch.

The Delta Grill, it turns out, is quite a find. Southern cooking, as a rule, doesn't travel well. Why, nobody knows. Corn fades once picked, and magnolia blossoms wither in the northern air. But why can't you find a good chicken-fried steak in the world's premier restaurant city? Such was my complaint for years, until the faint ping of the Delta Grill registered on my foodar that night.

Not that the Delta Grill is the last word in southern cooking. It isn't. Some of the entrees are only so-so. Pork chops étoufée are thick and served with a strong, subtle brown pan reduction, but one was badly overcooked. The andouie stuffing that accompanied it was pretty dubious. The jambalaya was good but not great. A blackened, garlicky filet mignon was a pleasant surprise, although the garlic mashed potatoes were overseasoned almost to the point of toxicity.

But the real find at the place was chicken-fried steak, which immediately shot to the top of the very short list of New York renditions of that Arklatex standard. Like potato latkes or barbecue, chicken-fried steak is almost never done right in a restaurant. If you've had it in the Southland, a pounded, breaded cube steak sautéed in lard and covered with a greasy, peppery white gravy, you can never forget it. But you seldom get it like that. Generally, most restaurants will deep fry a hamburger, coat it with white gravy from a jar, and call that chicken-fried steak. But "chicken-fried" isn't just an Applebee's-style adjective; it's a specific method speaking to the lore of southern cookery, with its omnipresent cast-iron skillet and singular cooking techniques. (Who else in the world deglazes roasting pans with coffee?) And the cube steak, for all its gray blandness, is still a steak. No matter how much they beat the hell out of it, there's still a texture resilient enough to stand up to some of the heaviest gravy the world has to offer.

The Delta Grill's chicken-fried steak is light, wide, and airy, with a true cube steak under a white onion gravy. It's not traditional, and I had to season it liberally with black pepper to get it the way I like it, but the onions put an extra element into play that fits right in. That's my idea of fusion cooking! And yet, the chicken-fried steak isn't really meant to be improved upon— it's one of those primitive but majestic parts of America, like rodeo or the Everglades. Still, the Delta Grill's version is pretty much the best I've had in New York, with Virgil's more traditional but too-massive version a close second.

Dylan Prime

62 Laight St. | 212.334.4783

💰💰💰

Meats of Note: carpetbagger steak

TriBeCa, the oldest part of Manhattan, has at all times in its history been a capital of gastronomy. Dutch traders ate well here in the 17th century; in the 19th century, Gilded Age gourmands like James B. "Diamond Jim" Brady kept opulent Broadway restaurants like Rector's in the black with their legendary fouteen-course meals. In our own time, TriBeCa is more or less the exclusive preserve of sleek media-business millionaires—its representative restaurant being Robert De Niro's TriBeCa Grill, two or three of whose typical customers could fit into Diamond Jim's pants.

Dylan Prime, then, is what you might expect from a modern TriBeCa steak house. The place is large and elegant, gorgeously designed with an austere sensibility. Plenty of open space, soaring ceilings, and lighting as artistic as an exhibit at the Guggenheim. The large bar area is littered with supermodels and the smashed aspirations of the men who would seek to get their phone numbers. (A fair number of high-bourgeois diners are present as well, usually in groups of three or four.)

Likewise, the food at Dylan Prime strives after a sophistication not to be found in more old-fashioned steak houses. Chef Bobby Duncan, a protégé of Gramercy Tavern's Tom Colicchio, is exerting his creative energies on his own restaurant for the first time. "I wanted it to be more like a restaurant," he told me, "and less like a steak house. I want to have more composed dishes; I want us to be more than just red meat." I suspected then that his heart wasn't really in beef, but I was curious as to what creative vectors he might take. This is a man, after all, who has served apprenticeships in Taillevent and the French Laundry, and whose mentor is widely regarded as the supreme exponent of the New American cooking.

Duncan's menu is in fact quite thoughtful and imaginative. There are composed dishes, like his "Carpetbagger Steak," a filet stuffed with Blue Point oysters and a sauce with Guinness, brown sugar, and shallots. It's an excellent dish, one which speaks to Duncan's southern background (he's from Savannah) and his training at Gramercy Tavern. But it's not something a cook with a beefy heart would have as a signature dish. Likewise, Dylan Prime's steaks, though of the highest quality and always cooked exactly to order, are a little undersized by traditional steak house standards, and come with a variety of extraneous sauces and baked-on "chapeaux" like Maytag Blue Cheese and chive, or wild mushroom and truffles. This effort to gild the lily is forgivable in a young chef, eager to spread his wings; but for an old meat-man like Mr. Cutlets, it's a regrettable, if understandable, urge. Less easy to condone is the influence of Collichio, who has now spread to his acolytes the anarchic business of letting customers choose their own sauces and accompaniments. Collichio has devoted a whole restaurant (Craft) to this pernicious practice, encouraging every shmeggege to be his own chef—and where will that lead? Mr. Cutlets patronizes a restaurant because the chef knows more than I do; if I wanted to create my own meal, I would go to the supermarket.

Still, Dylan Prime is an excellent restaurant on the whole, and far superior in atmosphere and appearance to most steak houses. Many of the composed dishes are magisterial, and New York foodies would do well to get in on the ground floor with Bobby Duncan. Following a talented young chef through his career is an especially satisfying thing—like watching a great prep-school basketball player blossom into a college star and then ascend through the pro ranks.

Elvie's Turo Turo

214 First Ave. | 212.473.7785

Meats of Note: Panay pork chops (Wednesday only), kare-kare

"Turo Turo" means "point, point" in Tagalog, the musical tongue of the Philippines. Mr. Cutlets, though, doesn't even need to point; when I come in on a Wednesday afternoon, experience has taught the friendly man behind the cafeteria counter to present me with Elvie's Panay Pork Chops. While Elvie's other dishes, such as pancit (soft noodles studded with pork) and kare-kare (tender chunks of oxtail, beef tripe, and mixed vegetables in peanut sauce served with salted shrimp paste) are good, they pale before her pork chops.

Meaty and marinated with a delicate brine, they're thickly breaded with a seasoned batter and served straight up with rice. For a couple of dollars more, you can have pancit on the side instead. But it's all about the pork chops! Residents of Alphabet City are accustomed to seeing Mr. Cutlets walking euphorically down East 12th Street, a pork chop held aloft in one hand. Although the fatty outer ridges of these chops are a delight in themselves—I often nibble around the edges as I walk, as with a macaroon—the meat inside is lean and firm. It makes an ideal Atkins snack or a protein-packed pick-me-up for the man or woman on the go; add in some of Elvie's excellent adobos and other delicious dishes, and you will be simultaneously immobilized and energized. Why Elvie makes them only on Wednesdays is beyond me; but it provides a helpful anchor in Mr. Cutlets' chaotic world, and for that I am grateful.

Five Points

31 Great Jones St. (bet. Lafayette St. & Bowery) | 212.253.5700

💰 💰 💰 💰

Meats of Note: pork chop, rib-eye steak, oxtail

Five Points is in every way a fashionable restaurant. It has a peerlessly hip location in the best part of NoHo, right off a stretch of Lafayette Street that includes such ultra-sophisticated venues as Fez, Joe's Pub, and the Public Theater. (The Blue Man Group, at the nearby Astor Place Theatre, is by comparison as hokey as a road company of Cats.) The clientele is equal parts downtown hipsters, gay, and otherwise, and the middle-aged beau monde. The restaurant is tastefully elegant, with a long, murmuring elevated canal bisecting it. It's not a place you would think of as a meat citadel. But then the pork chop comes out, and all doubt is dispelled.

Five Points' pork chop is truly a thing of beauty. (Although not, as Keats thought, a joy forever. It lasts only a few minutes.) Its bone arches along the curve of the plate, long and delicate. The meat is a round tower of grilled porkfection, no less than an inch thick and covered with the cross-hatched sear marks of the kitchen's flames, black against the honeyed color of the chop's sweetish glaze. This is some of the finest pork around, and Five Points handles it perfectly, cooking it precisely to the point when it loses pink color, but before it begins to dry out—which is always a threat with contemporary pork loin. The best part of this pork is its unexpected salty-sweet taste, with its hamlike undertones. This pork chop has been carefully brined, you realize, which is important, since it's so thick that you taste the meat a lot more than you taste the glazed and grilled surface.

Other dishes at Five Points to please the meat-needy palate include the grilled Black Angus rib-eye steak, garnished with a restrained chimichurri, and an elegant appetizer of braised oxtail, served with an oven-baked egg with plenty of yolk and some crisp bread on which to spread them both. The latter appetizer isn't for everybody, however; non-meat-mad diners would probably be better advised to order the razor clams. Desserts are great too, particularly the chocolate bread pudding served in a warm puddle of crème anglais.

Five Points is one of those restaurants where meat people can go with their more civilized spouses and still eat with abandon. It's a fair bet that the downtown glitterati won't even notice.

Kang Suh

1250 Broadway (at 32nd St.) | 212.564.6845

Meats of Note: short ribs, rib-eye steak

Manhattan's Korean section is the most self-contained of its many ethnic enclaves: it amounts to one block crammed with Korean restaurants, spas, and travel agencies, many piled

two or three high. Unlike most such concentrations, however, this jumble of activity doesn't seem to owe much to indigence. Nearly all the restaurants are large and richly appointed, with an affluent clientele from all over. And nearly all offer some version of Korean barbecue, which is generally done at your table. The biggest, and I think the best, of these is Kang Suh. Other restaurants are more beautiful than Kang Suh, and some are more accomplished with seafood and other Korean specialties. But when it comes to tabletop grilling, Kang Suh made a believer out of me.

I was skeptical, you see. Having many times cooked my little meat-pieces on the butane flames of these grills, I had assumed that it was merely a pleasingly interactive gimmick, like fondue, or those restaurants where you pick your own lobster out of a tank. And it is—when the fuel is gas. But Kang Suh actually sends an overheated man out from the kitchen with a basket of burning coals. They aren't napalm-soaked briquettes, either, but real hardwood lump charcoal. Prior to this, a constellation of condiments and chutneys arrives, circling the space where the coals will go. The people of Korea are the all-time champions of pickling, and these kim chi are a perfect counterpoint to the meats to come.

The meats are marinated for a long time in a complex brew of soy, wine, sesame oil, garlic, and God knows what else. The golgi, or short ribs, are thicker, headier, and more self-sustaining in the cross flow of flavor between smoke and spices; I thought it stood up better than did the bulgogi, or steak—in this case, thin, ruby slices of good rib eye. In either case, the meat was great, the cooking a happy diversion, and the kim chi refreshing between the multiple helpings of freshly grilled red meat that are the restaurant's raison d'e-tre. Who needs a whole Koreatown? Kang Suh is more than enough Korea for me.

Katz's

205 E. Houston St. (at Ludlow St.) | 212.254.2246

Meats of Note: pastrami, salami, hot dogs, corned beef

Katz's has three signs, representing three different eras in its illustrious history. On the long, brown wall facing Ludlow Street, "wurst fabric" echoes faded Yiddish back onto now-

SANFORD LEVINE > KATZ'S OWNER

uncomprehending streets. Today's punk-rocking population, paying $1,500 a month in trustafarian scrip, doesn't understand German, much less Yiddish. The neon "Katz's Delicatessen" sign on the Houston Street side, with its forties swankiness, is easier for them to appreciate. My favorite of the three signs, though, is the vertical, red-on-white incandescent "KATZ'S," which towers over the front door on the corner of Houston and Ludlow. That was my signal, as a child walking double-speed to keep up with my father, that we were almost at the promised land, that vast and magical place where my own father had been taken by his father, in his turn, a lifetime earlier. The hanging salamis, the ancient counterman with his sharp-hooked pinky ring for deftly cutting apart hot dogs, the clatter of plates, and the busy work of carving knives filled me with wonder and awe. Even as a child, I could feel the continuity between my father's childhood and my own, at least in this one magical spot; today, old and alone, I see it unchanged from my own first visit, and never see it without a pang of loss and nostalgia. The cavernous, bright interior, with its beer signs, its long cafeteria counter, the wood walls and old-time water dispenser, act on me like Proustian signifiers, bringing me back to a world I never knew, except by blood inheritance. And yet Katz's continues to make new acolytes, even as it moves forward in time. Twenty and forty years from now, adults will be explaining to their own children to hold on to the ticket given them at the door, to be marked in grease pencil in lieu of a check; and those children will instruct their own on how to tip the counterman a dollar (or whatever the currency of the future may be) to get a bigger, fresher sandwich, and a little taste of the meat served up on a saucer.

Happily, the restaurant seems blissfully unaware of its place as a fixed point in the universe. Katz's is the consummate New York deli; and yet, it has never sunk into parody, as have some of its uptown competitors. The last great deli in the last great Jewish neighborhood in New York, it has earned, through eminence and longevity, the right to advertise itself as a time machine; but it would rather just go on selling hot dogs. That

these are the best you can get goes without saying; the only way to improve on them is by eating the knockwurst, which are bigger and therefore better, and never more so than when brought home and grilled. The salami remains gnarled, garlicky, and fragrant; the pastrami and corned beef the best under the sun, and carved by hand into thick and irregular slices, making for a far more robust, coarse mouthful than the paper-thin, middle-loaded meats cut by the spinning blades of electric slicers. The french fries, which overflow lit-

KATZ'S PASTRAMI SANDWICH

tle white saucers behind a sneeze guard, are wide and brown; each portion contains a few preciously drenched fries, translucent with the taste of salty oil. Half-sour pickles and Dr. Brown's black cherry soda complete the experience, although great fressers have been known to top off a meal with an egg cream.

In recent years, Katz's has even made a few improvements. The boring black T-shirts have been replaced by a series of funky, downtown designs; menu items like chopped liver, beef stew, and potato latkes have been added. The "Send a Salami to Your Boy in the Army" sign is still in full effect, but now Katz's ships to places like Afghanistan and Sudan, where salami is unknown. And while the egg cream, that elixir, is still made with the traditional Fox's U-Bet, you can have pie or cake with it too. But everything that matters remains the same; there's even a painting of David Tarkovsky, whose hook-ring figures sank into so many customers' first, best memories. And the slogan remains the same: "Katz's, That's All." An accident—a printer put down verbatim what a harried owner told him—it just seems right so many years later: final, authoritative, absolute. This is the New York deli, now and forever.

Keen's

72 W. 36th St. (bet. Fifth and Sixth Aves.) | 212.947.3636

Meats of Note: mutton chop, prime rib hash

New York's steak houses generally fall into three categories.
There are the high-concept, art-directed new restaurants,
such as Dylan Prime, the Strip House, or City Hall, which fea-

MUTTON

ture modernist glosses on steak, and whose appetizers and
side dishes are often brilliantly original. Then are the old-
time beef baronies, the stark, unadorned, history-laden insti-
tutions to which all serious meat-eaters must eventually
repair. The prototype of these is of course Peter Luger, but
old-school avatars dot Manhattan; and among their number
is Keen's. In between are a number of faux-antique steak
houses, whose scotch-and-cigar aesthetic reflects marketing more than meat, and whose foods are indistinguishable
from casinos and cruise ships. But how can you tell the second type from the third? Generally, you find it in the unexpected detail.

Keen's, for example, dates back to the days when long-bar-

KEEN'S SIGN

reled briar pipes were smoked in taverns, itself a throwback to the auld sod of Ireland. The regulars at Keen's kept their pipes on a rack, and as the restaurant became famous, the powerful and celebrated sought to keep a signed pipe there; it was like having a star on the Walk of Fame. (Now, of course, rappers and sitcom stars have pipes on the rack; but what can you do?) Fortunately, a long-stemmed pipe collection has not yet arrived as a ready-made cliché for the design teams employed by today's corporate steak house franchises.

Likewise, every place has some kind of porterhouse for two; but how many restaurants feature a mutton chop as their signature dish? Keen's lists this unloved article at the very top of its menu, calling it "Our Legendary Mutton Chop" and charging $35 for it. Hardly anybody even knows what mutton is anymore. And yet Keen's must sell a few every night, to aging gluttons such as myself. Mutton is the meat of sheep; lamb is its immature form, bearing much the same relationship as veal has to beef. In every way, the flavor of mutton is more powerful, more pungent, and more robust than lamb, and the Keen's chop shows it at its best. A thick loin chop is one of the milder cuts of mutton, but the gamy piquancy still comes through—particularly in the crunchy fat that wraps the chop. Mutton is the kind of food people eat who never heard of mango chutneys, and whose idea of an appetizer was another mutton chop. It is one meat that knows its own taste—which is more than you can say for a lot of the beef you see, including Keen's.

One exception to Keen's rather generic beef deserves mention. Keen's serves a lot of prime rib, and as a result has plenty of scraps left over; this gets made into a delicious hash, which is browned up and served with a fried egg on top. The meat is completely well done, but it's still tender, coarse-cut, and unmistakably beefy, a perfect accompaniment to a burdened businessman's consolatory pint after work. It's a fairly recent innovation, but like everything else at Keen's, it has an aura of permanence about it.

Knickerbocker
33 University Place | 212.228.8490

$ $ $ $

MarkJoseph Steakhouse
261 Water St. | 212.277.0020

$ $ $ $

Meats of Note: porterhouse steak

How little of life can be judged by appearances is a question fit for deeper men than Mr. Cutlets. Generally, my own opinion is that appearances count for a lot. But the separate performances of two downtown restaurants provide a reminder that appearances can be deceiving.

Knickerbocker, on University Place at Ninth Street, is a genuine rarity—a bastion of high bourgeois culture, completely oblivious to the arms races of the 21st-century restaurant world. As a locale, it belongs entirely to the wealthy, middle-aged clientele who live nearby, who are more than happy to sit back and enjoy substantial old-fashioned meals while listening to unobtrusive jazz. Knickerbocker specializes in a kind of cooking that would not be out of place in the Gilded Age, albeit ornamented by a few modernist flourishes. (The oyster pan roast is served with artichokes in a vermouth-sage "nage," for example.) All this being the case, Knickerbocker is not the kind of restaurant you would expect to be exceptional. But such is the power of evolution in our time that Knickerbocker now boasts not only a menu worthy of Jim Brady, but one that is also as good as many of the finest steak houses around.

The chief proof of Knickerbocker's surprising power lay in a dish that every serious steak house attempts to define itself by: the sliced T-bone for two or more. (Technically, Knickerbocker can't call this steak a porterhouse because a big fillet is not always present.) Knickerbocker doesn't make any grand claims for this steak, nor do they age it a single day. "No, it's basically just dipped in a bit of soy, salted and peppered, and thrown on the grill," Jordan Schehr, Knickerbocker's manager, told me. "It's really just a basic preparation." The steak arrives in the familiar platter, propped up on one end to let the precious bodily fluids pool at the bottom, where two heavy tablespoons are provided as ladles. The steak is magnificently flavorful, tender, and full-bodied as only the best beef can be. Peter Luger is better; but I've had few steaks there that are as good as this one (and never at Smith and Wollensky). The Knickerbocker T-bone is also a great bargain: the single steak costs $29, but is more than large enough for ordinary people to share. The fine creamed spinach and the fat little crock of garlic mashed potatoes (or, alternatively, a football-size Idaho baker) are included in the steak's price, a departure from steak house convention. If there is a better short loin steak to be had in Manhattan, Mr. Cutlets doesn't know about it.

MarkJoseph Steakhouse, on Peck Slip near South Street Seaport, contrariwise presents itself as a tribute restaurant to Peter Luger; but the place should only be visited for academic reasons, or if someone else is paying. In nearly every regard, the homage paid by this yearling to its Williamsburg original is complete: there are crusty caraway rolls, sliced tomato and onion appetizers, the same awful red sauce in china gravy boats, the sliced porterhouse served on an inclined platter, with a pool of savory fat at the bottom. Even gruff, bald waiters have been recruited, or possibly grown from pirated stem cells. Sadly, however, the steak itself is utterly mediocre, as flat and bland as a piece of chicken at an Indianapolis Howard Johnson's.

MarkJoseph claims to share the same aging process as Peter Luger, but the product on the plate belies the hype. The steak has the unnatural tenderness and insipidity of wet-aged meat, the same stuff that is entombed in cryovacs and sent off to feed tourists in chain restaurants. MarkJoseph's saving grace, however, is its smoky-sweet Boar's Head bacon, which it slices half an inch thick and serves unadorned as a broiled treat.

The moral of MarkJoseph of course, is that appearances only matter to meat eaters for the meat it portends. There's nothing intrinsically attractive about gruff waiters and tilted plates; they serve to titillate the undiscerning; but the true gourmand knows in his or her bones that deathless motto, "Meat Matters Most." Knickerbocker is far closer in spirit to Peter Luger than its unworthy simulacra, however slavish its imitation. In meat, as in other matters of the heart, no lie can long withstand the clear-eyed glare of obsession.

La Dinastia

145 W. 72nd St. (bet. Columbus & Amsterdam) | 212.362.3801

💰 💰 💰

Meats of Note: pork chops, picadillo, spareribs

La Dinastia, like its more well-known rival La Caridad, is a specimen of that New York rarity, the Chino-Latino. Existing purely as a demographic accident (Chinese restaurants in

Puerto Rican and Dominican neighborhoods), they don't represent any kind of fusion: one side of the menu is Chinese, and the other Latin. Nonetheless, a hybrid vigor flourishes, and despite being Chinese-owned and operated, it is the Latin half of the menu that makes Dinastia special.

Consider the pork chops. La Dinastia serves not one but two different all-world versions of chuletas, or rather four, since both their broiled and fried versions are available as either loin or blade chops. Typically, the fried chops are better taken as blade chops; they are intersected by odd ribbons of golden-brown fat to complement the gorgeous gold crescent of their curving rims. (The serving is also pleasingly asymmetrical since the blade chops are weird shaped things and no two come alike.) The broiled chops, which are flawlessly meaty and moist, cooked to a T every time, are at their best as loin chops. These are the conventional all-lean chop sold in most restaurants, with the only fat a single thin boundary at the outside. The broiled loin chops are given a temperate fire, enough to cook them through but not enough to give them the Midas treatment the fried chops get. As a result, the fried chops look better to the eye, but the broiled chops are more substantial and satisfying.

Other outstanding dishes at La Dinastia include Picadillo, the classic Caribbean mix of spiced ground beef and peppers or beans, which most Americans experience in degraded form as chili or Manwiches. This Picadillo is good enough to eat straight up, although the yellow rice it is served atop absorbs it appetizingly. Better still are La Dinastia's spareribs, which are meaty, sizzling hot, and served without the sweet gummy goo, equal parts ketchup and honey, that ruin so many Chinese ribs. There is a sweetish-red char siu coating, but just enough to keep it sapid. They're also marvelously resilient and firm without being tough. Committed meatarians might try the ribs as an appetizer before getting the pork chops; a meal like that truly is "hog heaven."

L'Impero

45 Tudor City Place | 212.599.5045

🝰 🝰 🝰 🝰

Meats of Note: short ribs, roasted kid

L'Impero is a sleek, posh restaurant located in Tudor City, an elevated enclave near the United Nations. The crowd is international, tending toward early middle age. In short, it is a

solid, if unexciting, restaurant. And yet, it presents a four-course lunch that is all skyrockets and whistles.

I came to L'Impero for the roast baby kid. The goatlet is the kitchen's signature dish, and I felt that no meat guide could be complete without at least one capretto. And in fact, chef Scott Conant's braised capretto is a fine rendition, with reddish, al dente pieces of meat piled lushly together over a bed of firm fresh green peas. Unfortunately, the dish falls short in a few areas: the peas are too firm, and there's not much play to the piquant goat, which is appetizingly gamy, but not much else. But L'Impero features the aforementioned four-course lunch menu, and the other three dishes were all more exciting than the goat. Long slices of short ribs were exquisitely soft, supple, and rich, and served atop a risotto-like faro, itself studded with peas and tiny cubes of carrots. Beneath it all was a deep sauce so good that I held up the next course while I waited for the bread man to make a return trip. Afterwards came braised duck and foie gras agnoletti, a mere six or seven, but as potent as mescaline. (If this was how they ate in Escoffier's day, they must have practically been foie gras themselves.) The cheese course, which you would do well to take in lieu of dessert, features three separate cheeses, each with a special accompaniment. Old parmesana-reggiano came with a few precious, syrupy drops of 12-year-old balsamica modena, and firm peccornino with brandied walnut paste. It's all good, and the triangular little carafe of house red is too.

Lunch at L'Impero was an unexpected thrill in such a staid and obscure area. It will make you feel like a kid again!

Macelleria

48 Gansevoort St. | 212.741.2555

$ $ $ $

Meats of Note: bistecca fiorentina

The name Macelleria means "butcher shop," and given its location in the meat market, its perforated-steer logo, the immense cow head that is mounted on its back wall, and the meat hooks which hang on both sides of the restaurant, you would guess that the place is primarily concerned with the production of Bistecca Fiorentina, the definitive Italian steak. But no. Macelleria's menu does not preoccupy itself with steak. There are a number of very good pasta dishes like the chestnut ravioli, various ragus, creative appetizers, as well as an excellent wine list.

Just because it isn't glaringly obvious, it doesn't mean that Macelleria has spared any effort in the steak sweepsteaks. Their meat, superbly marbled and aged, is bought personally at the Hunt's Point meat market. This got me thinking. Why would a restaurant in the dead center of the meat market buy their meat in the Bronx? The meat right around the corner at Walmir is good enough for Peter Luger. Is it therefore a question of cost? These things are worth thinking about, since Macelleria is almost as expensive as Peter Luger. And as at Peter Luger, the steak is served two ways. There is the big porterhouse for two ($56), which comes sliced into thick pieces and served on the bone; and a large shell steak ($26) which is served with its tail, and is big enough to feed any man, and maybe a child besides. Both steaks are marinated with a little olive oil and some herbs, and broiled under intense heat.

The quality of the meat compares favorably to practically all of the best New York steakhouses, and you can even detect, particularly if you let it cool down a little, the extra zotz, the telltale twist of flavor that aging imparts to great meat. Of the two steaks, I thought the strip better. The porterhouse is so thick that eating it is a lot like eating roast beef; by that I mean that it suffers from a low interior-to-surface ratio. (The thickness also prevents it from absorbing much flavor from its marinade, not that it needs it.) There's something not quite there, however, about the steak; it doesn't sing. (Maybe it's the Brooklyn in the meat?) Also, Macelleria made the cardinal error of making both steaks medium, when one was ordered medium rare. Their medium, however, is a true medium, "all pink in the middle" as they say.

Desserts are excellent, though less so than you might want after a big steak dinner. An apple pie was terrific, chocolate gelato was very good, but the house chocolate cake was strictly from hunger. All in all, I liked my experience at Macelleria a lot; and while not the top of the top, I would go there again.

Maloney and Porcelli
37 E. 50th St. | 212.750.2233

$ $ $ $

Meats of Note: pork shank

Alan Stillman, one of New York's beef barons, has created an empire of midtown steak houses, including Cite, Smith and Wollensky, and the Post House. Cite is probably the best, but

all three are very fine steak houses. Still, it always rubs Mr. Cutlets the wrong way when copies are mistaken for their originals. Smith and Wollensky, for example, has aped its betters so successfully that even some unsuspecting food writers have been buffaloed into believing it some kind of definitive New York steak house. It isn't; it's just another very good chain, albeit one that spends a lot of money on looks, gift steak knives, and other tokens. (Stillman admitted as much to the Wall Street Transcript, claiming decor as the chain's most distinguishing characteristic.)

It's fitting, then, that the best restaurant in the Stillman group isn't technically a steakhouse at all, but rather the sui generis meat palace Maloney and Porcelli. Like all the restaurants in the Stillman group, Maloney and Porcelli serves very good beef; but the real standout here is the magnificent pork shank. It's hard to overstate just what kind of impact the Maloney and Porcelli pork shank has when it arrives at your table, a knife imbedded all the way to the hilt in its luscious flesh; even the most bright-eyed of gluttons might qualm at eating it whole. It can be done, but why try? By the time you've eaten the crisp golden skin with its delicate cider glaze and some of the pudding-tender pork underneath, complemented by braised sauerkraut dusted with poppy seeds, you've had a completely satisfying pork experience. Eat a plate of hash browns and have a beer, and take the remaining eight pounds of pork back home with you, to brown up with eggs the next morning. And the morning after that. And the morning after that . . .

Nebraska

15 Stone St. | 212.952.0620

💰 💰 💰 💰

Meats of Note: veal chop, rack of lamb, steaks

Steak houses, as a rule, all tend to market themselves the same way. The place is presented as a sanctum sanctorum, an all-male preserve where men can drink whiskey, eat charred beef, and revel in their temporary liberation from the tyranny of women. In New York, it should be even better, as history crowds in upon you in the form of ancient photographs, lore, and thick outer-borough accents. However, too often New York steak houses are depressingly generic, with "gourmet" menus and overpriced wines constituting the totality of the experience.

Which is why Nebraska is such a find. This is one of the great New York steak houses; why would it, then, have a name like Nebraska? And yet, this marketing misstep has had a salutary effect: anybody willing to go to the restaurant's two out-of-the-way locations is bound to be a serious steak eater, drawn there by word of mouth. The Wall Street location is literally on Manhattan's first paved street, and the restaurant in the Bronx is like something from a movie set. Both get a fair amount of business—the Bronx from local families, and Wall Street from young stockbrokers who are drawn there by the buxom bartenders and massive steaks and chops. But tables are easy to get at both restaurants after 8 p.m., and the prices compare favorably to most of the high-end steak houses in New York.

As far as the definitive steakhouse virtue, massive portions of magnificent beef, lamb, and veal, Nebraska has almost all of them beat. The veal chop in particular is a monument to artistic gluttony. A good two inches thick, it is slowly broiled for fifty minutes until the exterior is the color of tarnished brass, and the interior a juice-suffused expanse of pale pinkish-white. To complete the effect, the chop arrives end up, resting on the T of its huge bone. (Alfred Portale himself wouldn't be able to teach Nebraska anything about vertical platings.) The porterhouse is, without exaggeration, a full four inches thick; the rib eye a great broad slab of a steak, crusty, bloody and delicious. As I waded through this sea of meat, it occurred to me that the costs of such plenty much be prohibitive; but owner Pete DeMarco waved away my objection. "I'm a lousy businessman. Economically, I do everything wrong here. But I want everything to be great. It isn't complicated. I just serve what I like to eat." This commendable attitude even extends to the lunch menu, which features a big steak sandwich entirely of filet, and a huge, peppery ground sirloin under rich caramelized onions.

Given how grossly gratifying the meats are, you might expect the appetizers and side dishes to be similarly elemental. But DeMarco, whose youth was spent eating at the legendary Harlem Italian restaurant Rao's, serves some of the most refined appetizers you are likely to see in a first-class steak house: sautéed shrimp with pungent, briny garlic sauce; dense smoked trout with capirs and a delicate mustard dressing, and a fabulously fresh mozzarella caprese, served at room temperature, the way it was meant to be. The sides, too, at Nebraska are generous and inventive, other than the disappointing hash browns. A trio of sautéed peas, proscuitto, and onions is terrific, as are the creamed spinach and the sautéed broccoli rabe. The desserts are likewise opulent and intense, particularly the amaretto tiramisu and the handmade gelati.

As I ate this wonderful Italian steakhouse meal, I had to wonder why it wasn't better known. Nebraska is plainly in the same league with Macelleria, Tuscan, and the city's other top Italian steak houses, and is much better than many iconic but overrated New York meateries such as Gallagher's, Ben Benson's, or the Old Homestead. Whether it's the name, the location, or just the absence of marketing hype, the place doesn't get the attention it deserves. But for anyone that loves meat, it should.

New Green Bo

66 Bayard St. | 212.625.2359

Meats of Note: soup dumplings

Siu lim bao, or "tiny juicy buns," are one of the best things that have happened to Mr. Cutlets since the Versailles treaty. A regional specialty of Shanghai, they aren't generally found in most Chinese restaurants—any more than you would find a bialy in "American" restaurants overseas. But Shanghai cuisine is coming on strong, and at its vanguard are siu lim bao, the potent soup bombs that are its most identifiable specialty. Joe's Shanghai is bigger and more famous, but the Shanghai invasion was begun by New Green Bo, and it remains my favorite. The chow fun (broad noodles) with shredded pork and preserved cabbage are a perfect take-home reward for jury duty well discharged, and New Green Bo's magenta-hued pork belly, served with savory greens, is almost enough to inspire a hasty "guilty!" ballot.

But the real draw here is the soup dumplings. They are the size of a handball, white, and come by the dozen. They arrive on a bamboo steamer, and are surprisingly heavy when you pick them up, owing to the thick broth and meat inside, and the heavy walls needed to contain it. Novices are often burned badly when they eat their first soup dumpling, because the soup inside is scaldingly hot and rushes out into your mouth at first bite like Marx Brothers bursting out of a stateroom. A wiser course is to puncture a dumpling with the end of a chopstick and squeeze a little soup onto a spoon while the rest cools. As good as the seasoned ground pork inside is, it's the soup that's the real draw. This precious fluid is dense with taste, fat, and that mysterious ingredient that 18th-century gourmands called osmazome. "It is osmazome," declared Jean Athelme Brillat-Savarin, the Aristotle of eating, "which constitutes the real merit of good soups." This "eminently sapid" substance, which Brillat-Savarin credited science with identifying after a thousand generations of blissful ignorance, has been the subject of great con-troversy among food scientists, some of whom consider merely as collagen, and other as completely imaginary. Whatever it is, it seems to have something to do with those parts of the animal that dissolve into soup, leaving nothing behind them but a thickened stock. The soup thus enriched takes on a substance and body which owes little to fat, and less to muscle. Gluey, transparent, and transporting, it car-ries a wallop which doesn't diminish. Shanghai soup dumplings prove that what we love in meat doesn't neces-sarily inhere in the muscle, or even the bone; though its fats and flavors are explained by science, and elevated by cooks, the mystery yet remains.

Niko's Medditerraneo
2161 Broadway | 212.873.7000

Meats of Note: leg of lamb, rotisserie pork, lamb chops, kabobs, mousakka

As the lengthy "meats of note" above might suggest, there's a lot for meat-people to like about Niko's. In fact, as the directing intelligence of not only Niko's, but also Big Nick's Burger Joint and the Burger Joint Too, Nick Imiriziades might be said to be among the heroes of Meat Me in Manhattan. The New York media, though, continues to underappreciate him. The Times' Eric Asimov, one of the city's most estimable critics, had this to say about Niko's: "[Niko] tries to head upscale here, but the result is hard to differentiate from a diner, with its enormous menu, emphasis on Greek dishes and generic execution." While I put much stock in Asimov's judgment, I think he missed the point. It's exactly because Niko's is a glorified diner that it is great.

The Greek diner is the bedrock of restaurant food in America, and one who doesn't like diners doesn't like American food. This is especially true of Greek diners, which have the oldest provenance of America's diner traditions, and whose Mediterranean-inflected menus are most citizens' first gateway to foreign cooking. A boy's first moussaka is a crucial an event as a junior prom, and stays with him all his life. Niko's, as a restaurant, represents the Greek diner raised to its highest level. There is a vast menu, immense portions, a crowded and noisy atmosphere, and elemental tastes in plentiful supply. Really, the sensibility isn't that different from Ouest, the "comfort food" citadel a few blocks up Broadway. These are basic tastes that know their own mind, are made from good ingredients, and which are improved by an uncommon care and a little bit of imaginative tinkering. In Niko's case, that translates to an almost-unprecedented success level with lamb, one of the city's most neglected meats.

Niko's leg of lamb is a Sunday special even more successful, on its own terms, than Ouest's meatloaf. The meat is slow roasted on the rotisserie and arrives on a vast platter, the lamby, fragrant, ultra-moist meat flanked by soft string beans braised in tomato, Greek style oven roasted lemon potato, rice pilaf, and garnished with tsatsiki and mustard. It's easily enough to feed two, but then someone would have to miss out on Niko's wonderful clay-pot dishes, such as the lamb shank with orzo and tomatoes. Again, the comparison to Ouest comes to mind. These shins aren't in Tom Valenti's class, but they are served so simply, with such inevitability, that it's hard not to think of them as preexisting in the universe. The orzo absorbs the lamb and tomato flavors, becoming as substantial as risotto, and liberal amounts of dusted cheese, carrots, and peas round out what might be the perfect "comfort food" when all is said and done. Then there are the loin lamb chops angelo, thick and savory and bearing the hot marks of the grill under their potent rosemary and lamb-reduction sauce.

For lunch, Niko's serves a fine, thick beef hamburger, plus 25 other terrific dishes, but my favorite is the souvlaki, or the leg of lamb "shish kabob," which the menu mouth-wateringly describes as "Generous cubes of leg of lamb, on a skewer with onion, pepper, and tomato. Grilled over the char-wood fire. Splashed with ladolemono marinade. Served with rice pilaf and garnished with roasted beets." Yes please! Likewise, the rotisserie pork is nearly as good as the lamb, and like all the sandwiches, comes with a colorful bouquet of crisp fries, yam fries, and ultra light breaded eggplant strips. Sitting in Niko's, drinking a tall glass of iced tea or cheap Greek wine, you realize that Niko's, like the Greek American diner, isn't so much a restaurant as a way of life.

Old San Juan

765 Ninth Ave. (bet. 51st and 52nd Sts.) | 212.262.6761

💰 💰

Meats of Note: churrasco, mofungo

The Old San Juan, in Hell's Kitchen, and its sister restaurant in Gramercy, are the best (and only) Puerto Rican/Argentinean hybrids I know of in New York City; but, for my money, they're all you need. Neither restaurant is much to look at, especially the one on the West Side. But in an area where many very good, very inexpensive restaurants cluster, Old San Juan is one of Mr. Cutlets' favorites.

Why? Because with its two highly meat-centric sources, Old San Juan is a terrific, economical resource for meat-eaters on the West Side. Take their mofungo, for instance. For under $10 you get a colossal portion of this Puerto Rican national dish, which is garlic-infused smashed plaintains mixed with fried pork rinds. Mofungo is the kind of dish you could eat on a Monday and still be full on Wednesday. It's not for everybody, but if you like it, this is the place to get it. Old San Juan's Argentine side is best represented by its churrasco, the marinated skirt steak which is the signature dish of Argentine grilling, and the mixed grill, which includes both the churrasco, pork sausage, and blood sausage. The churrasco at Old San Juan is juicy, crusty, big, and cheap. Two people would do well to split it and one of the excellent seafood sopas, paellas, or shrimp dishes, which the restaurant also does a great job on.

Pampa

768 Amsterdam Ave. (bet. 97th & 98th Sts.) | 212.865.2929

💰 💰

Meats of Note: grass-fed beef

Mr. Cutlets, in this helpful guide, has endeavored only to present restaurants which he can vouch for. I can't write about every restaurant; this book would be as heavy as a bowling ball. So I stick to sure bets. But occasionally I eat in a restaurant which really gets me thinking, and Pampa is one of them. It therefore makes an excellent platform for a topic that has perplexed me for years—What's the deal with grass-fed meat? I'm often asked this question, and I'm at a loss to answer. By rights, grass-fed cattle, such as are corralled on the plains of Argentina, should be superior to our own chemical-gorged, hormone-injected, ultra-processed products. Grass should give them a distinctive taste, an organic élan different from cattle forced to subsist on spiked grain mix. And of course all that walking around on the grassy pampas should help too. Certainly, that's the way it's presented to us by marketers of the wholesome beef, and not a few reputable meat-eaters have testified to its excellence.

Mr. Cutlets, however, just doesn't see it. The grass-fed beef that I've bought from Fairway market, and other very good butchers, has never been as good as even an average steak of comparable price; and the grass-fed beef I've eaten in restaurants has, if anything, been even worse. Part of it may be due to the greater leanness of Argentine cattle; that's bound to depress the quality of any meat. But even the basic taste of grass-fed beef seems weak. Far from having a distinctive, feed-informed flavor, it mostly tastes like a weak solution of American beef. Maybe it tastes better in Argentina; it wouldn't be the first export that was scandalously inferior to its original. Just think of Mexican food. But here, at least, Argenentine beef just doesn't cut it.

Take Pampa. This popular restaurant on the Upper West

Side, though a bit run-down looking, continues to pack customers in for their signature grilled meats. It is relatively inexpensive. But the grilled short ribs are tough, sinewy, and taste like nothing so much as the "swiss steak" they fed you in junior high. The skirt steak, which is considered the star of the menu, looks good, and releases a lot of juice onto the plate. But, to quote Gertrude Stein, there's no there there—no earthy oomph, no skirt-steak succulence, no vivid beef-blood flavor. There's not much of anything, and so customers have to resort to spooning on the potent garlic mojo, which serves the same purpose of A-1 sauce in places like Tad's Steaks. If this meat is better than American beef, then Mr. Cutlets needs to be in another line of work.

Pan Pan

500 Malcolm X Blvd. (at 135th St.) | 212.926.4900

  Ⓢ

Meats of Note: fried baloney, sausages, scrapple

Mr. Ben Barrow, the good-humored proprietor of Barrow's Pan Pan, was originally born in North Carolina, and like his countryman Charles Gabriel (see page 51), has adopted the great iron skillets of home as symbolic of good cooking. Pan Pan, a busy coffee shop across the street from Harlem hospital, features simple Carolinian short order cooking of a kind you don't find just anywhere. That, Mr. Barrow explains, is the idea behind the restaurant's name.

"Pan Pan goes back to when everything was cooked in the pan," he says. "They didn't have the modern things we have today. Meat, fish, bread—it was all cooked in the pan." Pan Pan is a fully equipped restaurant, though. "We use modern things now. We have the grill, and the fryolater. We have pots! [He laughs] We don't just have a pan. All the utilities that go into running a restaurant, we have. But we still make things the way they used to when we had our restaurant in North Carolina."

The original Pan Pan was on route 85 in Durham, but Mr. Barrow moved it to Harlem in 1977, and the place has become something of an institution, at least in the neighborhood. The low, orange counters that snake along the restaurant's length always seem to be full, and there is usually someone waiting for a take-out order. The most popular items are the sausages, which come in both beef and pork varieties, and the fried baloney sandwich, a thick slice of crusted lunchmeat served on a white enriched bun. (You have to ask for the thick sandwich; otherwise you would just get a sliced fried baloney sandwich, which you could get anywhere.) The sausages, like Mr. Barrow and his cooking culture, are imported from North Carolina. The beef sausages come in both mild and hot varieties, but it's the pork sausage that really works—especially when served with scrambled eggs and grits.

Of course, if you're going country, you would do well to order some scrapple too. Not many places in New York serve scrapple, one of the few remaining meat products which openly boast of originating as offal. The faces, ears, livers, and so forth that constitute scrapple are finely ground and mixed with sage, pork broth, and cornmeal, and formed into a cube, which you can slice up and cook, presumably in an iron pan. (Scrapple, I think, is unlikely to ever be embraced by New Yorkers. You can see that from a recipe from a cookbook I own, which begins, "Take a stiff wire brush and clean the snout thoroughly.") Pan Pan's scrapple is nice and brown and thick, and goes well with grits and little glasses of orange juice. Mr. Barrow doesn't put much stock in worrying about trans-regional tastes, though. "It wasn't a North Carolina thing," he explains. "We just had it down there. Now, we make it up here. So, it's a New York thing."

Note: Pan Pan will be adding outdoor seating soon—a big boon, given how hot it can sometimes get inside.

Pio Pio

1746 First Ave. | 212.426.5800

                                     $

Meats of Note: rotisserie chicken

Pio Pio, we are told, is the sound a chick makes upon first emerging from its egg. A bittersweet note, you would think, given the restaurant's practice of slowly roasting the animals, and then feeding them to people. But no! Euphoria, rather than regret, is the dominant mood here.

The rotisserie, of course, is probably the most perfect engine of meat-cookery yet devised. The meat waltzes slowly around the fire, its hot juices oozing alluringly as they bake back onto the sizzling skin. Meat pulls from the bone as the inexorable process continues, the muscle soft and moist beneath the twice-seared skin. Add some exotic spices and a skillful marinade, and you've got the makings of a perfect meal. Probably the best rotisserie chicken in the five boroughs is Los Pollitos II, on Fifth Avenue in Brooklyn; but Pio Pio is the best in Manhattan, narrowly beating out the west side's excellent Flor De Mayo and a number of other very fine restaurants.

The key is the marinade. Pio Pio leaves their chicken immersed in Peruvian beer and spices for twelve hours, and serves it, split and unadorned, as the main item on their short menu. A whole chicken costs $10, and is a thing of beauty. It's more than enough for two, particularly when accompanied by the fruity house sangria and a plate of starchy, salty, and delicious French fries. (Skip the yucca frita—it's too big, too dry, and not crunchy enough to beat out the fries.) The whole meal at Pio Pio, for two, shouldn't come out to more than $25, including sangria. The room also happens to be clean and cheerful, a pleasant place to sit even without the chicken. But once you're eating the chicken, you can see why they would want to celebrate its birth. (Though the restaurant's mascot, a winking chick, can be a little disconcerting.)

Savannah

7 E. 48th St. | 212.935.2500

Meats of Note: rib-eye steak, pork chop

The vogue for traditional steak houses exhausted itself some time during the late 1990s; as the genre flourishes in the aughts, it has already begun to branch and mutate. Circa 2003, the feminized steakhouse is in many ways the quintessential venture. Why cut out half the population, the thinking goes; and elegant beef-centric restaurants have been opened by the likes of David Glazer, Terrence Brennan, and Jean-Georges Vongerichten in recent months. Savannah belongs to this school. A soaring midtown space marked by a stark black-and-white design motif, the place is so littered with models and actresses that you could cut yourself on all the cheekbones. A respectable share of the clientele also consists of corpulent men there for the generous meat dishes and innovative sides. The appetizers are especially luxuriant: a dark and glittering tuna tartare, a deep bowl of delicately-battered calamari, and a pyramidal tower of steak tartare are the best among them.

Among the entrees, a spiced rib-eye steak stood out, and the pork chop had a salty-sweet delicacy that comes from careful brining. A macaroni-and-cheese soufflé tower, at least visually, was the best of an assortment of artful side dishes. Savannah is up against tough competition: within a few blocks, one can eat at Cite, Ben Benson's, Angelo and Maxie's, Gallagher's, Maloney and Porcelli, and of course Smith and Wollensky. But the restaurant, staff, customers, and foods are all attractive; and among the new breed of steak houses, that might be more than enough.

Sparks Steak House
210 E. 46th St. | 212.687.4855

Meats of Note: New York strip steak

Sparks Steak House, unfairly, owes the better part of its fame to the 1985 assassination of underworld boss Paul Castellano outside its doors. The celebrated hit elevated

John Gotti to the preeminent position in the mob, and Sparks to iconic status; but the latter would have been deserved anyway. Sparks is, along with Peter Luger, the prototypical New York steak house.

The place looks like a cross between a social club and a brothel. Frosted glass panes with an "S" protrude from every booth, and the walls are covered with dozens of—as far as I can tell—indistinguishable landscape portraits of trees in winter. The waiters are helpful without being overly familiar. (They don't tell you their first names.) The menu is straight from 1949: lump crabmeat, prosciutto and melon, and shrimp cocktails to start off, and then steak, veal chops, lamb chops, and a few broiled fishes. All in all, it seems like the kind of place where a Mafioso should meet his end. But that doesn't mean you shouldn't go there for other reasons.

Take the sirloin steak. Sparks' sirloin steak is actually more accurately a shell steak, or New York strip. It's a narrow steak, dry-aged a long time, and a good inch thick. It arrives on a bare plate. The top is blackened evenly, having charred underneath the hottest of all gas broiler flames. There are no grill marks. There are no spices. There is no garnish, no sauce, no chutneys; there isn't even, as in Peter Luger, a pool of melted blood and butter to spoon on. (I put a little butter, left over from the bread, on top, with some black pepper and a scattering of salt, just as accentuators.) What there is is the mineral sharpness that comes with only the very best aged beef—that elemental, briny elixir. But what really makes it special is that char, the sizzling, dark-brown surface with its few but precious sections of sizzling fat along the tail. This steak has the density (and commensurate depth of flavor) you would expect from aged shell steak; you need to use your knife to cut it, and your jaws to chew it, and you're glad you did. Only a vegan could prefer the mushy blandness of tenderloin. If you don't like this steak, you just don't like meat!

The hash browns also deserve special mention. They're my favorite, and they participate perfectly in the virtues of the steak. They aren't as crusty as you might hope, and the portion isn't big enough for two to share. But the taste of butter is complete upon them, extending all the way through their light, dry, potatoey insides. Most restaurants parboil their hash browns, which leaves them heavy and waterlogged, and keeps the taste of butter from ever absorbing; that's why, on mediocre hash browns, the only taste is in the heavy crust. But these are mealy, Idaho-style potatoes which have obviously been baked ahead of time. Baking is a dehydrating process—it leaves a still-starchy, airy vehicle for butter, and packs these hash browns with salty-fatty oomph.

There are a number of other first-class dishes at Sparks. The triple-thick lamb chops, especially if ordered butterflied, are among the best I've ever had; and the veal chop is fit for a Cardinal. But you would have to be out of your mind to order anything but the sirloin steak. If you find yourself at Sparks in a larger party, you could always get the lamb chops as an appetizer, split three or four ways. This would gratify gluttony and gregariousness—a rare confluence, and one welcomed by even the most hardened of eaters.

Waterfront Ale House

540 Second Ave. (at 30th St.) | 212.696.4104

Meats of Note: chili, buffalo steak, beer sausage, game

It may be hard for New Yorkers to appreciate how bad food is everywhere else. Let's say you live in Big Flats, New York or Mishawaka, Indiana. If you want to go have a beer and some

thing to eat, in most cases you're going to end up at a franchised "family" restaurant with stop signs on the walls and ten different kinds of nachos. It's sad stuff, but what can you do? As with a hasty marriage or a go-nowhere job, a resigned laugh is all the world allows by way of consolation. In a better world, eating at bars would be something to look forward to. Rather than peppy girls reciting ad copy, and portion-controlled "fun foods," you would eat handmade German sausages, and an imaginative cook would supplement a reliable, creative menu with half a dozen different meat specials every night. The place would be small and out of the way, so that it could cater to knowing regulars, and unpretentious, so as to fly beneath the radar of foodies.

That better world can be glimpsed, here and now, at the Waterfront Ale House, in Kips Bay. The place benefited early on from low expectations: prior to the opening of the huge movie theater across the street, the corner was as remote and depressing a location as you could find in midtown—two blocks from the projects and one block from Bellevue. But the friendly bar staff and the better-than-needed kitchen kept the regulars coming in.

Ralph Yedinak, the Waterfront's chef, is a big man who looks and sounds a lot like the Yankees' David Wells. Unlike most of the better chefs in New York, Ralph started out with an Associate's Degree in Wisconsin, and then was a straight-up journeyman for ten years before taking the reins at the Waterfront Ale House. Here, he had a free hand to develop the menu. "I love to come up with new things," he says. "My regulars come in and they go straight to the specials board." His regular menu items are inventive enough—a beef chili buttressed with sweet pulled pork, for instance, or a Shaller and Weber wurst trio (bock, brat, and bauer) platter. Even Ralph's standards are a little special—his French dip sandwich is served on crusty, buttery garlic bread, and his spareribs are tender, delicately smoky, and dusted with a bold Memphis-style rub.

But Yedinak really lets himself go with the specials. No one considers the Waterfront Ale House a temple of fusion cookery, but Ralph is willing to try anything that sounds interesting to him. On just my last two visits, specials included chicken braised in chimay ale, cumin-rubbed rib-eye steak with port-chive butter, flank steak on mushroom sobu noodles, and salmon seared in rice wrappers. With so much going on, there's bound to be a few misses (in this case the rib steak), but overall the food is surprisingly refined and totally satisfying. I'm not saying the Waterfront Ale House is better than Union Pacific or Eleven Madison Park, but it has a lot more in common with those places than with most bar menus.

The other thing Waterfront Ale House is known for is its commitment to game meats. "In Wisconsin, we hunted a lot and there was a lot of game meat around. So that's something we try to do here a lot," Yedinak says. Every night, the specials board includes two or three game dishes: an ostrich burger, buffalo steak with cumin-coriander ketchup on the side, or (another time) with a dollop of truffle butter melting on top. (The last was the best thing I ever ate at the Waterfront Ale House, and made me wish "the big shaggies" still covered the plains.) Venison is always well represented.

Ralph Yedinak can flat-out cook, and even if you just want a sandwich and a beer, you could hardly do better than the Waterfront Ale House. Now if only they would open 4,000 new locations.

Note: The Waterfront Ale House has a sister restaurant in Brooklyn, which Ralph Yadniak is not involved with.

Acme Bar and Grill
9 Great Jones St. | 212.420.1934

💰 💰

A poor man's Five Points; stop in for pecan-grilled
pork chops and chicken-fried steak.

Agean
221 Columbus Ave. | 212.873.5057

💰 💰

Better-than-it-has-to-be; Greek features include
dynamite baby lamb and grilled quail.

Alison on Dominick
38 Dominick St. | 212.727.1188

💰 💰 💰 💰

The menu changes frequently, but for years it's been
one of the most consistently creative of American
restaurants, with a sure feel for hearty meats.

All State Cafe
250 W. 72nd St. | 212.874.1883

💰 💰

Tiny, quiet, out-of-the-way restaurant with one of
New York's better hamburgers, and superior fried chicken.

Angelo and Maxie's
233 Park Ave. | 212.220.9200

💰 💰 💰 💰

Slightly generic steak house has huge portions of
fine meat in fun surroundings. Only obsessive
steak connoisseurs could complain.

DB Bistro Moderne
55 W. 44th St. | 212.391.2400

💰 💰 💰 💰

Boulud's sleek theater-district bistro, home of the
ludicrous DB burger, but also magnificent steak,
boeuf en gelée, pork chops, guinea hen, and pig's trotters.

BB Sandwich Bar
120 W. 3rd St. | 212.473.7500

                                                    💰

Cheesesteak specialist worth visiting, but not
worth waiting in line for. 100 others are just as
good, more or less.

Blue Ribbon
97 Sullivan St. | 212.274.0404

                                          💰 💰 💰 💰

Tony restaurant known as chef hangout.
Oysters are special, the fried chicken less so.

Bouterin
420 E. 59th St. | 212.758.0323

                                          💰 💰 💰 💰

Provençal stalwart with a sure touch for meat—
seven-hour leg of lamb, for instance.

Cabana Carioca
123 W. 45th St. | 212.581.8088

            💰 💰

Cheap theater-district meatery features immense,
garlicky steaks, chicken, and feijoda. Great for
parties and no-frills bachelor feeds.

Cafe Con Leche
424 Amsterdam Ave. | 212.595.7000
726 Amsterdam Ave. | 212.678.7000

                               💰

Can be counted on for delicious chuletas con mojo
(pork chops with garlic sauce), ground beef empanadas,
and ropa vieja (shredded beef). Great breakfasts, too.

Cafecito
185 Avenue C | 212.253.9966

                              💰

One of the few first-class Cuban places in Manhattan,
and it's cheap, too. Look out for fabulous Vaca Frita
(braised and grilled flank steak).

Campagna
24 E. 21st St. | 212.460.0900

Mark Strausman's Italian "comfort food" is
unambitious and hearty, yet refined.

Christine's Polish American
208 First Ave. | 212.254.2474

No-frills Polish diner produces magnificent cutlets—
how could I not love it? Breakfast sausages are
worth getting up early for.

D'Artagnan
152 E. 46th St. | 212.687.0300

Foie gras arcadia: stop by for four-course duck
menu, or a Leaving Las Vegas-style goose liver binge.

Delmonico's
56 Beaver St. | 212.509.1144

Financial district expense-account soak; not
really worth the price. A relic of the Gilded Age of
interest only to the historically minded.

Etats-Unis
242 E. 81st St. | 212.517.8826

Superb restaurant; worthy of a longer review.
You won't be disappointed, with dishes like veal
chop in mushroom sauce, beer-braised short ribs,
and Niman Ranch pork dishes.

Fairway Cafe
2127 Broadway | 212.595.1888

Add-on to legendary market; BYOB steak dinners;
T-Su are a real bargain.

Fiorello's
1900 Broadway (Lincoln Center) | 212.496.2471

 $ $ $ $

Doubleplusgood veal parmesan, thick and vivid.
As Virgil "The Turk" Sollozo says, "Try the veal;
it's the best in the city."

Frank
88 Second Ave. | 212.420.0202

 $ $

Superb, ultra-fresh Italian food; one of the city's best.
Look for meat loaf and various special ragus.

Gramercy Tavern
42 E. 20th St. | 212.477.0777

 $ $ $ $

One of America's great restaurants, and a legitimate
meat mecca, too. Go for their roasted rib steak
with braised short ribs, foie gras, and
potato gratin. Boo-yeah!

Heidelberg
1648 Second Ave. | 212.650.1385
Old-school German, with plump wursts.

Island Burger
766 Ninth Ave. | 212.307.7934

 $

Toppings verge on farce, but the hamburgers
and shakes deliver.

Kurowycky Meat Products Inc
124 First Ave. | 212.477.0344

First Avenue Meat Products
140 First Ave. | 212.777.4583

 $ $

Nearly indistinguishable Ukranian meat stores
on adjoining blocks of the East Village. Both
feature a wide variety of homemade kielbasas,
house-smoked bacons and hams, and many
hard-to-find specialty meats, at modest prices.
The "home-style" ham (the big one in the window)
is especially wonderful.

La Fonda Boricua
169 E. 106th St. | 212.410.7292

East Harlem Puerto Rican, specializing in mofungo and chuletas. "I eat here every day, mang. It's always good," one man told me. He's right, too.

Lawrence Scott
1363 First Ave. | 212.396.4555

Superb, underappreciated restaurant—the Peacock Alley of the aughts. Scott trained at Lucas Carton and Restaurant Louis XVI, both Michelin 3 stars. All-world lamb shank and more.

Le Veau D'Or
129 E. 60th St. | 212.838.8133

Heavy, old-school Alsatian bistro: charcroute, cassoulet, coq au vin. Sauerkraut with lard is nice, too.

Leshko's
111 Avenue A | 212.777.2111

East Village hipster hive; may be too, uh, gay for some, but it makes great burgers.

Lupa
170 Thompson St. | 212.982.5089

Mario Batali's greatest creation, for Mr. Cutlets' money. Inexpensive, brilliant versions of fried pork shank, oxtail, lamb sausage, braciole, saltimbocca . . . and that's without even mentioning the salamis. Pastas are just fantastic.

Mercer Kitchen
99 Prince St. | 212.966.5454

Downtown outpost for Jean-Georges Vongerichten's brilliant cooking. Hard to say if the models or the ginger-braised short ribs are more attractive.

Merge
142 W. 10th St. | 212.691.7757

💰💰

West Villager known for red-sauce "Sopranos"
Sundays; better than you might expect.

Michael Jordan's Steak House
Grand Central Terminal | 212.655.2300

💰💰💰💰

Don't be fooled by the name: superb
steak house located inside Grand Central Terminal
is one of New York's best.

Miss Mamie's Spoonbread
366 W. 110th St. | 212.865.6744

💰💰

Thoughtful and reliable southern soul food.
Sloooow service and bantam-sized portions
are major drawbacks, though.

Molyvos
871 Seventh Ave. | 212.582.7500

💰💰

The best Greek restaurant outside Astoria
(not that I had better there).

Moustache
265 E. 10th St. | 212.228.2022

💰💰

Addictive, understaffed Middle-Easter.
A rare source for lamb ribs.

Nha Trang
87 Baxter St. | 212.233.5948

💰

Vietnamese phô specialist: heady brews of tendons,
rice noodles, and beef broth.

Nice Restaurant
35 E. Broadway (bet. Market St. & Bowery) | 212.406.9510

One of the best dim sum houses in town:
rolling cars of tasty appetizers circulate a busy
room. Save room for squab, black bean rib tips,
salt-packed chicken, and suckling pig.

Old Homestead
56 Ninth Ave. | 212.242.9040

With its old-time credentials, meat-market
location, and giant cow out front, you want it
to be great. But it's not even good.

Old Town Bar
45 E. 18th St. | 212.529.6732

Classic old-timey New York bar featuring the
city's best-loved chili dog. Great atmosphere,
too, esp. when it's slow.

Palm
837 Second Ave. | 212.687.2953

Famous but underperforming steak house.
Good but not great. Not much fun, either.

Pasha
70 W. 71st St. | 212.579.8751

First-rate Turkish restaurant. Marinated grilled
quail is good, but lamb chops rule.

Pesce Pasta Trattoria
262 Bleecker St. | 212.645.2993

Known for their wide range of fresh seafoods, but
the veal chop keeps Mr. Cutlets coming back,
as does the wonderful lasagna bolognese.

Pig Heaven
1540 Second Ave. | 212.744.4333

                                    💰 💰

Plenty to squeal about at this pork-themed
Chinese. Pig ear salad and other rare dishes
make for a change of pace.

Pomodoro Rosso
229 Columbus Ave. | 212.721.3009

                                    💰 💰

Busy Columbus Ave. eatery with an outstanding
Fiorentina (T-bone) for two.

The Post House
28 E. 63rd St. | 212.935.2888

                               💰 💰 💰 💰

Another Alan Stillman steak house, less glitzy
than Smith and Wollensky or Cite.
Solid and dependable.

Prune
54 E. 1st St. | 212.677.6221

                💰 💰 💰 💰

Refined, ingenious cooking, from duck breast
"pastrami" to roast capon to marrow toast.
Should be a girly restaurant and yet its aesthetic
is almost Cutlets-esque.

Romeo's (formerly Zito's East)
211 First Ave. | 212.475.4500

                                         💰

Best of the old-time coal-oven pizzerias, especially
the meatball pie. Fresh-mozzarella people may
prefer Lombardi's.

Ruby Foos
2182 Broadway | 212.724.6700

                                    💰 💰

Large, dark, beautiful, and noisy pan-Asian.
Tamarind ribs always put a hop in my step.

Salumeria Biellese
378 Eighth Ave. (at 29th St.) | 212.736.7376

Sets the standard for salamis and soppressatas.
Stop here before any camping trip or bicycle tour.

Second Avenue Deli
156 Second Ave. | 212.677.0606

Good chicken soup and chopped liver, but the
pastrami's better in Cincinnati. One of the
all-time marketing jobs. Don't bother.

Silver Spurs
771 Broadway | 212.473.5517

490 LaGuardia Place | 212.228.2333

Hamburgers are big yet disc-shaped; cheese
is yellow and bacon is plentiful. And they deliver.
What more do you want?

Smith and Wollensky
797 Third Ave. | 212.753.1530

Overrated and generic, but undeniably excellent
steak house. Ask for the Colorado rib steak
(not on the menu).

Stage Deli
834 Seventh Ave. | 212.245.7850

Ben Ash, Artie's, and Fine & Schapiro are all excellent too.

Steak Frites
9 E. 16th St. | 212.463.7101

Dependable rib steak for two, with frites, and a bacon
salad to start with. Way-hot clientele is a bonus.

The Strip House
13 E. 12th St. | 212.328.0000

                                      💰 💰 💰 💰

Elegant and inventive, but at the end of the day,
the steak doesn't stand out.

Terrence Brennan's Seafood and Chop House
565 Lexington Ave. | 212.715.2400

                                      💰 💰 💰 💰

Breakfast of champions: marrow toast with
smeared braised rib. If only they made it in the
morning. Few entrées excite, though.

Union Square Cafe
21 E. 16th St. | 212.243.4020

                                      💰 💰 💰 💰

A contemporary classic; deserves its enormous
popularity. The bar burger at lunch is a special
treat, though too big for Mr. Cutlets' taste.

Vince and Eddies
70 W. 68th St. | 212.721.0068

                  💰 💰

Underrated American with consistently fine
cooking. The steak seldom disappoints.

27 Mr. Cutlets' Prayer

ON the long road of life, the journey's full of bumps,
Troubles, and viscissitudes, and a man must take his lumps.
Women bear the burdens of a thousand daily cares;
And disaster may at any time strike us unawares
But let us now be happy, at least while we eat
That's Mr. Cutlets' prayer, for people who love meat

Let your beef be always bloody,
and your soul as white as veal;
May your pork be pink and salty
With nothing wasted but the squeal.

May your sausage always be plump,
and your chicken always crisp,
May your stews and daubes be unctuous,
nourishing, and rich.

Let your table always be covered
With the thickest steaks and chops
Let those who would restrain you
May themselves be stopped.

Let your bacon be well-cured,
As a kindly tended patient,
May your palate not get bored
Nor your restaurants complacent.

From Harlem to the Battery
On sidewalk or on street,
May Mr. Cutlets bless you,
Wherever we may MEAT.

Restaurants appearing in guide

21 Club
21 W. 52nd St.
btwn Fifth & Sixth Aves.
212.582.7200
B, D, F, Q to 50th St. 🚇

26 Seats
168 Ave. B
btwn 10th & 11th Sts.
212.677.4787
L to First Ave. 🚇

Acme Bar and Grill
9 Great Jones St.
btwn B'way & Lafayette
212.420.1934
6 to Bleecker St 🚇

Agean
221 Columbus Ave.
at 70th St.
212.873.5057
1, 9, 2, 3 to 72nd St. 🚇

aKa Café
49 Clinton St.
btwn Stanton &
Rivington Sts.
212.979.6096
F to Delancey St 🚇

Alison on Dominick
38 Dominick St.
btwn Hudson & Varick
212.727.1188
C, E to Spring St. 🚇

All State Cafe
250 W. 72nd St.
btwn B'way & West End
212.874.1883
1, 9, 2, 3 to 72nd St.;
B, C to 72nd St. 🚇

Angelo and Maxie's
233 Park Ave. at 19th St.
212.220.9200
4, 5, 6; L; N, R, W to Union
Sq.; 6 to 23rd St. 🚇

ápizz
217 Eldridge St.
btwn Stanton &
Rivington Sts.
212.253.9199
F to Delancey St. 🚇

Artie's Deli
2290 Broadway
at 83rd St.
212.579.5959
1, 9 to 86th St. 🚇

Artisanal
2 Park Ave.
at 32nd St.
212.725.8585
6 to 33rd St. 🚇

Balthazar
80 Spring St.
btwn Broadway &
Lafayette St.
212.965.1785
6 to Spring St.; N, R
to Prince St. 🚇

BB Sandwich Bar
120 W. 3rd St.
(MacDougal St.)
212.473.7500
A, C, E; B, D, F, V to
W. 4th St. 🚇

Beacon
25 W. 56th St.
btwn 5th &
6th Aves.
212.332.0500
E, V to Fifth Ave.;F to
57th St. 🚇

Beppe
45 E. 22nd St.
btwn Broadway
& Park Ave. South
212.982.8422
6 to 23rd St. 🚇

**Big Nick's Burger and
Pizza Joint**
2175 Broadway
btwn 76th & 77th Sts.
212.362.9238
1, 9 to 79th St. 🚇

Blue Ribbon
97 Sullivan St.
btwn Prince &
Spring Sts.
212.274.0404
C, E to Spring St.;
N, R to Prince St. 🚇

Bombay Harbour
72-32 Broadway,
Queens
718.898.5500
E, F, G, R, V to
Jackson Heights/
Roosevelt Ave. 🚇

Bouterin
420 E. 59th St.
btwn First Ave. &
Sutton Place
212.758.0323

Brother Jimmy's BBQ
1485 Second Ave.
btwn 77th & 78th Sts.
212.288.0999
4, 5, 6 to 77th St. 🚇

Cabana Carioca
123 W. 45th Sts.
btwn Broadway &
Sixth Ave.
212.581.8088
1, 2, 3, 9, N, R, W, 7 to
Times Square 🚇

Café Boulud
20 E. 76th St.
(btwn Fifth &
Madison Aves.)
212.772.2600
6 to 77th St. 🚇

Cafe Con Leche
424 Amsterdam Ave.
at 80th St.
212.595.7000
🚍 1, 9 to 79th St.;
B, C to 81st St.

726 Amsterdam Ave.
at W. 95th St.
212.678.7000

Cafecito
185 Ave. C
212.253.9966
🚍 L to First Ave.

Campagna
24 E. 21st St.
btwn Broadway & Park
Ave. S.
212.460.0900
🚍 4, 5, 6; N, R to
23rd St.

Carmine's
200 W. 44th St.
(Carmine's Midtown)
btwn Broadway &
Eighth Ave.
212 221.3800
🚍 A, C, E to 42nd St.

Carmine's Uptown
2450 Broadway
btwn 90th & 91st Sts.
212.362.2200
🚍 1, 9, 2, 3 to
96th St

Carnegie Deli
854 Seventh Ave.
btwn 54th &
55th Sts.
212.757.2245
🚍 A, C; B, D; 1, 9 to
59th St. - Columbus
Circle

Charles' Southern-Style Kitchen
2841 Frederick
Douglass Blvd.
Eighth Ave.
at 152nd St.
212.926.4313
🚍 D to 155th St.

Christine's Polish American
208 First Ave.
btwn 12th & 13th Sts.
212.254.2474
🚍 L to First Ave.

Churrascaria Plataforma
316 W. 49th St. btwn
Eighth & Ninth Aves.
212.245.0505
🚍 C, E to 50th St.

City Hall
131 Duane St. btwn W.
Broadway & Church St.
212.227.7777
🚍 A, C; 1, 9, 2, 3 to
Chambers St

Corner Bistro
331 W. 4th St.
Corner of Jane St. &
Eighth Ave.
212.242.9502
🚍 A, C, E to 14th St.;
L to Eighth Ave.

Cozy Soup and Burger
739 Broadway (Astor
Place)
212.477.5566
🚍 N, R to 8th St.
6 to Astor Place

Daniel
60 E. 65th St., btwn
Fifth & Madison Aves.
212.580.8700
🚍 6 to 68th St.

D'Artagnan
152 E. 46th St.
btwn Lexington Ave. &
Third Ave.
212.687.0300
🚍 4, 5, 6, 7 to 42nd St.
- Grand Central

Dawat
210 E. 58th St.
btwn Second &
Third Aves.
212.355.7555
🚍 4, 5, 6; N, R, W to
59th St.

DB Bistro Moderne
55 W. 44th St.
btwn Fifth & Sixth Aves.
212.391.2400
🚍 B, D, F, V, 7
to 42nd St.

Delmonico's
56 Beaver St.
212.509.1144
🚍 2, 3, 4, 5 to Wall St.;
N, R to Whitehall
St./South Ferry

Delta Grill
700 Ninth Ave. at 48th St.
212.956.0934
🚍 C, E to 50th St.

Dylan Prime
62 Laight St.
at Greenwich St.
212.334.4783
🚍 1, 2, 3, 9; A, C, E to
Canal St.

Ear Inn
326 Spring St.
btwn Greenwich St. &
Washington
212.226.9060
🚍 1, 9 to Houston St.;
C, E to Spring St.

Elvie's Turo Turo
214 First Ave.
btwn 12th & 13th Sts.
212.473.7785
🚍 4, 5, 6; L; N, R, W to
14th St.–Union Sq.

Etats-Unis
242 E. 81st St.
btwn Second & Third
Aves.
212.517.8826.
🚍 4, 5, 6 to 86th St.

Faicco's Pork Store
260 Bleecker St.
btwn Sixth & Seventh
Aves.
212.243.1974
🚍 1, 9 to Christopher
St.–Sheridan Sq.; A, C,
E; B, D, F, V to W. 4th
St.–Washington Sq.

Index

Restaurants by neighborhood

SENDA KATZ'S SALAMI

Who is Mr. Cutlets?

Mr. Cutlets is Josh Ozersky, the author of Archie Bunker's America:
TV in an Era of Change, 1968–1978 (Southern Illinois University
Press, 2003) and a frequent contributor to the New York Post.
Like Mr. Cutlets, he lives in New York City.